1973

This book may be kept

Crosscurrents / MODERN CRITIQUES

Harry T. Moore, *General Editor*

British Drama
Since SHAW

Emil Roy

WITH A PREFACE BY
Harry T. Moore

SOUTHERN ILLINOIS UNIVERSITY PRESS
Carbondale and Edwardsville

FEFFER & SIMONS, INC.
London and Amsterdam

Printed in the United States of America
Designed by Andor Braun
International Standard Book Number 0–8093–0579–8
Library of Congress Catalog Card Number 72–188699

Contents

Preface

Emil Roy's book on British Drama Since Shaw takes us further into the subject than earlier books in the same vein. Professor Roy's study does this because he includes the younger, advance-guard playwrights of the 1960s.

The title of this volume might lead some potential readers into thinking it deals only with playwrights after Bernard Shaw. But Shaw is very much a part of this book, whose first chapter is specifically devoted to him. The author puts Oscar Wilde into a second chapter, although he is usually considered as preceding Shaw. But Dr. Roy considers only one play of Wilde's, his comic masterpiece The Importance of Being Earnest, which dates from 1895, two years before the first publication of Shaw's not yet produced Widowers' Houses. Certainly Wilde's other theatrical writings, such as An Ideal Husband and Lady Windermere's Fan, are now interesting as only trivial period-pieces; even Salome is viable today only as the libretto of Richard Strauss's opera.

The third, fourth, and fifth chapters of this book deal with three other Irish-born playwrights, William Butler Yeats, John Millington Synge, and Sean O'Casey. Of these men, Yeats kept up his relationship with Ireland, although he spent much time in England and elsewhere, and O'Casey lived the last part of his life in England; but Synge, who like Wilde died prematurely, lived most of his life in Ireland; his youthful residence in Paris was an exception.

Professor Roy next takes up T. S. Eliot and Christopher Fry, to the second of whom he devoted a book published earlier in this series. But note how many of these men were playwrights only secondarily: Yeats and Eliot are the two leading British poets of the twentieth century. (It is proper to call Yeats, Synge and others, British, though they can hardly be spoken of as English; and Eliot is British too, for he was a British subject for more than forty years, although he can also be designated as English or Anglo-American.)

The last chapter of this book, entitled "The Moderns," takes up five of the more recent playwrights who are indisputably English: John Osborne, John Arden, Harold Pinter, Arnold Wesker, and John Whiting.

Now just what does the author do with all these men?

First, he sees them as representing two great ages of the British theater. The earlier of these is the one which began near the turn of the century, including Shaw and his contemporaries, while the second comprises the "moderns."

We read in the chapter on Shaw that this playwright cared less about his fame as an artist than as a social reformer, the man who wrote so many Fabian-slanted books and pamphlets. In Major Barbara (1905), Shaw writes paradoxically about munitions making, which is shown as a kind of evil benefaction. Andrew Undershaft, the manufacturer, is "a thoughtful man of action" who "reflects Shaw's deep ambivalence toward both authority and his own creative powers." Professor Roy points out something that emerges from productions of the comedy as well as readings of it: "The play's dominant tension between facts and values, between what is and what man wishes were so, is never provided with any definitive relationship to reality." Yet Major Barbara is a remarkable achievement, worthy of the several pages Dr. Roy devotes to it. He also gives a generous amount of space to such plays as Heartbreak House and Saint Joan, which represent Shaw at his finest. He "never failed to confront fantasy with at least the consequences of a rigid, apparently immutable social order," but "managed at his best to balance verbal fluency against the perils of futility, the desirable against the attainable." It is just such elements that keep Shaw alive in today's theater; the man once thought to be "dated" can still provide intellectual entertainment.

Professor Roy continues with a valuable examination of The Importance of Being Earnest, showing—technically as well as ideologically—why this is Wilde's best play by far. The author finds paradoxes in the theatrical writings of Yeats, as he did in the cases of Shaw and Wilde: his dramas contain "a compressed psychodrama of compulsion, presenting an irreconcilable conflict between transformation and identity, time and immutability." Beginning with The Player Queen ("Yeats's first successful play"), Professor Roy investigates the poet's work in the theater, at its best when Yeats accepts "his opposing selves, mask and creator" (using Yeats's own terms). In this discussion we are given an excellent, up-to-date projection of what Yeats did in drama, with myth, language, and technique.

In the chapter on Synge, Dr. Roy gets beyond the earlier critics who have said that Synge "uses all the devices at his disposal to adjust the claims of imagination to reason, fantasy to reality, the ordinary to the ideal." But this author sees instead that "although both are often victims, it is man against woman or, within the personalities of both, aggressive and acquisitive vs. passive, accepting tendencies." He provides a thorough and fresh consideration of Synge's great work, The Playboy of the Western World, but doesn't neglect that magnificent unfinished work, Deirdre of the Sorrows. He also finds an ambivalence in the "ideal and analytic drives" of O'Casey, singling out Juno and the Paycock and The Plough and the Stars for special discussion, pointing out how they are superior to the later plays. And, in his overview of Eliot and Fry, he deals expertly with the problems of modern poetic drama.

Emil Roy perceives the newest phase of the British theater beginning in 1956 with Osborne's Look Back in Anger. In many ways this final chapter is the most exciting in the book because it is largely a pioneering venture, dealing with the tensions of the five authors as they work toward their own kind of polarity. To say this is not to suggest that the earlier essays are in any way of lesser value: they have so many fresh insights that they are compelling to read. Professor Roy doesn't waste time on those who turn out what he calls the plays for "a middle-class theater of escape." In commenting so expertly on the principal playwrights since Shaw and Wilde, Emil Roy has produced a book at once important and highly readable.

HARRY T. MOORE

Southern Illinois University
February 29, 1972

Introduction

The resurgence of British drama at the end of the nineteenth century revitalized the theatre in a new but
characteristically traditional manner, John Russell Brown
points out. "It was so in Shakespeare's age, during the
Restoration, at the end of the eighteenth century, and
at the end of the nineteenth: and so, again, today." [1] In
the nineties the most creative theatre people were Anglo-
Irish, descended from an alien, imported ruling class with
little practical experience in acting, directing, or theatre
management. Writers such as Yeats, Wilde, Shaw,
Synge, and O'Casey lacked the firmly established, lav-
ishly subsidized theatres available at some point in their
careers to Ibsen, Chekhov, Strindberg, Pirandello, and
(quite late) Brecht. The problem of gaining popular
rather than official support involved struggling Irish
playwrights in competition with conservative, profit-
oriented and parasitic managements who welcomed
broad farce, spectacular operettas, and melodrama. Denis
Donaghue has described Victorian theatre, still with us
in new guises, as "confused, naive, often absurd, chaotic
—but in ways that reveal our own chaos," [2] and Francis
Fergusson has termed it, somewhat less charitably, as an
endless series of "commercially profitable shadows on
the cave wall." [3]

The most talented of the Irish playwrights were as
divided within as they were from their own countrymen.
Many emerged from broken, traumatized, *declassée*
families, seeing their homeland with the painful clarity

of "outsiders' outsiders." Unequipped with spontaneous, inborn traditions and feelings of heritage, men such as Yeats and Synge envisaged Ireland in an idealized mirror of English social customs, European culture, and Western history. Entering the theatre from apprenticeships in the novel, criticism, poetry, and the essay, Yeats and Shaw as well as their shifting groups of associates and disciples were forced to create, encourage, and direct small experimental theatres hospitable to new plays and train their own actors. Without exception, such theatres as the Abbey in Dublin and J. T. Grein's Independent Theatre in London failed to attract a steady flow of funds or innovative plays. Many were destroyed by success when a hit play was transferred to the commercial theatre, drawing most of the original company with it. Or they succumbed to the numbing effects of government subsidy or outworn tradition. Unfortunately, precious creative energy was often squandered on internal quarrels over form and intention between playwrights and hostile Irish audiences, as in the famous 1907 *Playboy* riots. Or writers clashed, culminating in the *Silver Tassie* controversy in 1928 between Yeats and O'Casey, in effect marking the end of early twentieth-century British drama.

A second wave of innovative, rebellious drama swept into the theatre in May 1956, with the production of John Osborne's *Look Back in Anger*. Conventional enough in its forms and traditions, Osborne's play paved the way for such diverse and talented writers as Harold Pinter, John Arden, Arnold Wesker, and John Whiting, among many others. The production of these writers (with the exception of Whiting, who died in 1963) and their associates continues with no waning in sight. No other nation in the world today, in fact, can equal the industry and inventiveness of Britain's living dramatists. In the book which follows, some of the most lasting contributions of England's (and Ireland's) more creative playwrights are considered in terms of their assumptions, talents, and literary vision.

I am greatly indebted to the Purdue Research Foundation which provided me with a 1970 XL Summer Grant to further progress on my study of modern British drama. I am also grateful to my wife Sandra for her unfailing tolerance and indispensable assistance.

EMIL ROY

Lafayette, Indiana
December 1971

British Drama Since SHAW

1

Bernard Shaw

Bernard Shaw's dominance of modern high comedy is undisputed, even though he consistently sought political and intellectual preeminence rather than artistic fame. W. B. Yeats's career in the theatre is equally as long, beginning and ending a decade earlier, and the attitudes of both are sharply divided between the utopian zest of the visionary statesman and the objectivity of the disinterested maker. Ironically, it is Yeats rather than Shaw who exhibits the growing self-mastery of the Methuselan Long Livers visualized by Shaw as the next-to-last stage of mankind's evolution toward spiritual purity, although his later stress on sensuality and decay counters Shaw's fix on the "higher passions." Yeats's contemptuous term for Shaw was "barbarian of the barricades," a phrase which probably fit Shaw's disciple and fellow expatriate Sean O'Casey more snugly, allowing for the exaggeration. Shaw is far more complex than detractors such as D. H. Lawrence, T. S. Eliot, or James Joyce would allow, but he deliberately underplayed his far greater success in the commercial theatre for the sake of reform, preachment, and moral impact. At the same time, Shaw's values were much more deeply rooted in the nineteenth-century currents of liberal skepticism than were those of most of his Irish contemporaries in the theatre. As a result, the growth of his fame as a European man of letters in the second and third decades of this century paralleled a decline in his influence as a

polemicist, socialist, and iconoclast. Yeats's monarch-
ism, which he expressed so markedly in the Cuchulain
plays which span his entire productive life, was more
retrospective and mythic than Shaw's, though it led to
similar disillusioned flirtations with fascism in the
twenties and thirties. And both men formulated and
amplified their theories of social improvement primarily
through societies of intellectuals, the press, and ap-
pointive office. However, Yeats's energetic acceptance
of rhythmic pendulations of growth, attainment, decay,
and dissolution in character, society, and history freed
him from Shaw's preoccupation with future social
betterment.

Sean O'Casey stands above Shaw's innumerable imi-
tators as the one talent with genuine originality. Few
slums appear in Shaw, only one play is set in Ireland,
no guerrilla warfare batters families apart, and though
both loved music, Shaw builds musical form into the
very structure of his plays, R. B. Parker notes,[1] unlike
O'Casey's interpolation of songs into the text. Both men
were functionally fatherless, resulting perhaps in the
ardent feminism both expressed through the vital sexuality of their heroines. And both men were socialists
sympathetic to communism, though with a Christian
and pacifist bent. Unfortunately, Shaw's influence appears most powerfully where O'Casey is weakest, in
his love of pseudopoetic diction, self-indulgent rhetoric,
and sententious epigrams. At his best, however, O'Casey
expressed more sympathy toward democracy than Shaw,
applied a similar distinction between vitality and
theories of vitalism which distances his poseurs, and
excelled in the comic argument of abuse.

Although O'Casey lacked Shaw's encyclopedic
grounding in Victorian social, economic, and political
thought, he was in harmony with Shaw's wider philosophical position, his so-called metabiology of creative
evolution. Shaw's views on a myriad of subjects from
eugenics to women's rights to profit sharing and dozens
of other problems poured forth in prefaces, statements,

pronouncements, speeches, and plays, the latter resembling veiled discourses addressed directly to the audience. In his prose Shaw is a straightforward utilitarian propagandist concerned with exhorting, stimulating, and reforming no less than the whole of society. Basically, Shaw argues that mankind has evolved not through chance and vicissitude, which entails a blind indifference and cruelty within man and nature, but through the mythic drive of a universal will he called the "Life Force" after Bergson's *élan vital*. For Shaw, although this force has both human and cosmic aspects, its main function is the improvement of man's moral and intellectual values. In a borrowing from Nietzsche, the hoped-for superman, somehow both part of a social group and above it, will be as superior to man as man is to the animals, replacing God. After a transitional stage of Long Livers, who have "willed" a saintly high intelligence along with a tremendous life span, the process will culminate in the disembodied "Vortices of Thought" implied in his antidramatic *Back to Methuselah* (1921). The philosopher C. E. M. Joad took Shaw's ideas seriously enough to provide philosophical equivalents for them, and Eric Bentley has written an admitted polemic for his ideas.

However, Shaw's concepts were derived less from scientific analysis than from his habitually cheerful temperament, resulting in a finely honed sensitivity toward likeness in dissimilars. "Given Caesar and a certain set of circumstances," he claimed, "I know what would happen." [2] Richard Ohmann has noted Shaw's passion for tight categories and exaggerated opposites, cliché juggling, paradox, discontinuity, the use of imperatives and interrogatives, and persons as representing attitudes. He has concluded that Shaw's

> quest for likenesses is a struggle to overcome through the organizing energies of mind, the threatening randomness of experience. In embracing discontinuity, on the other hand, Shaw rejects the me-

chanical tyranny of past over present and asserts
man's right to control himself and his world.[3]

Norman Holland has reached virtually the same point
through psychoanalysis, concluding that Shaw's basic
theme is the oral one of talking oneself loose from an
enslaving matrix (such as woman or the past) felt as
demeaning or threatening the very separateness of his
identity.[4] Shaw's programs for evolutionary reform take
their fervor and impact from the argumentative vitality
of his prose style rather than from originality of content.
Despite his disclaimers, he is unusually indebted to
"Schopenhauer, Nietzsche, Ibsen, Strindberg, Tolstoy or
some other heresiarch in north or eastern Europe." In
a Dionysian era swept by currents of unpredictable
change, Shaw's refusal to accept or even acknowledge
man's self-destructive passions has rendered his social
philosophy irrelevant, largely justifying Robert Brustein's conclusion:

> As a revolutionary doctrine, Shaw's ideology is un-
> original, unconvincing, and even rather timid; and if
> the world has remained indifferent to it as a program
> for salvation, then this, for once, has been for good
> and sufficient reasons.[5]

What really counts in his plays resulting in the tension
of engrossing conflict, is the passion with which his
characters identify their integrity with ideas, using talk
to dominate, neutralize, or fend off a threatening antagonist or idea.

Shaw's formal dramatic practice is admittedly traditional, marked by stock comic devices, ventriloquistic
personae, and a concern for the utilitarian functions of
literature. "My stories are the old stories, my characters
are the familiar harlequin and columbine, clown and
pantaloon; . . . my stage tricks and suspenses and
thrills and jests are the ones that were in vogue when I
was a boy." In contrast to O'Casey's increasingly simplistic stress on revolutionary activism, Shaw dropped

socialist themes early after *Mrs. Warren's Profession* (1893). His comedies typically match well-meaning but socially petrified functionaries against restless and vital ironists, collectivists against individualists, men against women. At the same time, his "Shavianizing" inverts melodramatic stereotypes. In repeated versions of the Venus and Adonis motif, Shaw stresses "the tragi-comic love chase of the man by the woman." They do so, in theory, not because they are driven by more powerful sexual drives than men possess, but because of a desire for motherhood. Since fatherhood absorbs so little of their creative interests and energy, Shaw's artistic men seek to escape into "higher passions" and therefore must be trapped into marriage. However, Shaw's women are ladylike, Victorian sophisticates driven by exceedingly genteel versions of the passions exhibited by Brecht's elemental women for children. And to the extent that Shaw's male protagonists succumb to marriage, they are proven both inferior to their women and inadequate to their own ideas.

In his drama Shaw avoids the poetic ambiguity of Yeats or Synge. Rather, he either adopts a classical irony in which his own views are unmistakable or balances incompatible values against one another with no references to nondramatic reality at all. With especial reference to *Major Barbara*, Francis Fergusson identifies his concept of action as rationalizing, "based upon the freedom of the mind to name and then to rationalize anything, without ever deviating from the concept to the thing." [6] Touchstones of reality, often personified in Moliere and Jonson by stable, down-to-earth folk, are usually missing. This may reflect the contempt Shaw unconsciously feels not only for bodily functions, but for the very nature of human existence Higgins expresses in *Pygmalion:* "Oh, its a fine life, the life of the gutter. Its real: its warm: its violent: you can feel it through the thickest skin: you can taste it and smell it without any training or work." With only occasional lapses, Shaw vigorously suppressed the notion found in

Yeats, Synge, and O'Casey at their best that the corruption and degradation of mankind would outlast the
most vociferous efforts at exposure and reform.

In his first two decades as a dramatist, from *Mrs.
Warren's Profession* (1893) to *Pygmalion* (1912), Shaw's
extremely varied production is based upon the same enlightened drawing room as Oscar Wilde's. As Eric
Bentley has observed,[7] the plays of the nineties are
chiefly simple inversions of current theatrical patterns,
such as Victorian melodrama (*The Devil's Disciple*),
the heroic play (*Caesar and Cleopatra*), and farce
(*You Never Can Tell*). From *Man and Superman*
(1901–3), he creates discussion drama (*Getting
Married*), dialectical drama such as *The Doctor's
Dilemma,* and fantasies like *Androcles and the Lion.*
Major Barbara (1905) is a representative example of
Shaw's early comedy. The play takes as its paradoxical
thesis, Fergusson points out, munitions making as the
path to salvation. On this basis, Shaw has parcelled out
logically incompatible platforms among all the characters: Lady Britomart's desire for both the Undershaft
money and the creed of the Church of England, Andrew
Undershaft's kindly wisdom and complete dedication
to destruction, and so on. As in Shaw's *Three Plays for
Puritans,* Undershaft serves as vital catalyst, disillusioning his daughter Barbara and converting Cusins, his
antagonist and Barbara's fiancé, into a mature unity of
knowledge and power, or so it seems.

The first act focuses on Lady Brit's attempt to force
her long-estranged husband Andrew to subsidize the
support of her adult children, about to marry, without
losing her influence over their decisions or their love
for her. The arrival of the munitions magnate to meet
his assembled family locks him and Lady Brit in a
strenuous, though well-mannered struggle for allegiance.
As in *King Lear*, each of the characters is forced to
weigh measurable facts against immeasurable values,
portraying inner struggles that mesh with the outer
action to bring each act to crisis.

Ironically, Undershaft's conflict with Lady Brit unveils the actual motives underlying her moral and his social rationales in an earlier crisis, the one leading to their separation. For beneath an artful pose of helpless incompetence, Lady Brit is a steel-nerved wheedler. Trying for a repetition of her successful squelch of her son Steven's bid for independence, she tries to force Andrew to "open up," to passively support the marrying children. As in marriage, it appears, her primary motive is a calculated drive toward entrapment, reducing a husband to personal and sexual powerlessness. Like so many of Shaw's vital characters, Undershaft experiences a racking tension between "being swallowed into a role or asserting oneself through words," in Holland's terms. Though he seems perfectly human, Undershaft appears passionless (symbolized by his functional bachelorhood), exhibiting the kind of cool, uninvolved self-control Shaw usually regards as diabolical. It is as though he had responded to Lady Brit's smothering maternality by repressing all positive feelings of affection and replacing them, in his devotion to armaments, with a child's furious fantasies of unbridled power. Striking a responsive chord in Barbara's sympathy for the poor and Cusins's collecting of religions, he remarks, "I am rather interested in the Salvation Army. Its motto might be my own: Blood and Fire." In a Shavian inversion, he proposes a bargain designed to shape the struggles of the following acts: he will visit Barbara's Salvation Army shelter if his family will accompany him, in return, to his munitions works. Wishing to control the action from a distance, Undershaft intends placing his charges in unanticipated crises to see how they will react.

In act 2 the noise and hyperbole of farce are crowded into an Army shelter. Bill Walker, a cockney *miles gloriosus*, has lost his girl to a converted wrestler. His attempts to bully the Army workers, fend off conversion, and finally buy salvation parody the gestures Undershaft enacts on a larger scale. The apparent success of the Army, like that of the Undershaft family, masks a financial crisis which Undershaft is asked to remedy. Sillier, though equally determined and maternal, Mrs. Baines succeeds brilliantly where Lady Brit had failed, disillusioning first Walker and then Barbara, who resigns her post. Labeling himself a "confirmed mystic," Undershaft poses as a divine conductor leading his spiritual children through a maze, showing them visions, and bringing them from illusion to reality, though his contempt for "the common mob of slaves and idolators" undercuts his objectivity.

The final act takes the Undershaft clan through the munitions works which, with its prosperity, stability, and religious trappings, resembles a socialist paradise. Ironically, it parodies a Catholic theocracy, its foundling directors inverting the childlessness of Popes, securing institutional above family ties. Despite Cusins's remark that "it only needs a cathedral to be a heavenly city instead of a hellish one," the virtues of the plant's employees are the sum of their collective defects: envy of superiors, contempt of inferiors, dread of a devastating explosion. An employee's reaction to a discarded match symbolizes the unstable combination of smoldering resentments beneath a cool, deceptively congenial appearance brought together in Undershaft's mock utopia.

A thoughtful man of action, Undershaft reflects Shaw's deep ambivalence toward both authority and his own creative powers. As uncomfortable as his creator when he "had to come out of the realm of imagination into that of actuality," he has withdrawn from the active sexuality and unremitting compromises of family life. Instead, he has entered the anthropomorphized, bisexual embrace of the munitions works where he could channel his untrammeled drives into the production of weapons. Not only his profession, but his delight in covert manipulation of others reveal a man who, beneath his icy self-control, seethes with an angry passion at everyone and everything. (Insofar as his cannons are long, cylindrical, and explosive, they are phallic symbols.) While he can indulge his hostility freely by selling armaments to all who can afford to buy, his strange passivity toward the works reveals covert feelings of guilt and inferiority: "It does not belong to me. I belong to it. It is the Undershaft inheritance." Part of his anxieties, of course, are shifted upon his gentle, unaggressive partner Lazarus. In return for indulgence of his fantasies, he has accepted emotional reduction from the works' master to its least significant part, a slave to time and punctuality, as Cusins remarks, "You do not drive this place: it drives you." Ironically, the heavy though passive demands of the works on him link them emotionally with Lady Britomart's more aggressive solicitations.

The last act reaches its crisis in the bargaining scene between Undershaft and Cusins. It revolves ironically around numbers which are meaningless not only to Cusins, regarding his salary and interest in the firm, but to us: the pounds going to the marrying children, the cartridges Cusins had given to a revolutionary student, the soldiers or dummies (interchangeable to Undershaft) blown up by new weapons. As a result, Barbara is supposedly converted to the salvation of contented workers, Steven Undershaft earns independence, and Cusins remolds his values, his profession, and even his name on Undershaft's model. Cusins's capitulation seems to synthesize Barbara's idealism and her father's realism at the expense of credibility and strength, ending the play in paradox. Whether he is defeated or converted, however, is unresolved. The play's dominant tension between facts and values, between what is and what man wishes were so is never provided with any definitive relationship to reality. Its carriage-trade conventions remain consistent and recognizable, but totally self-contained.

In view of *Major Barbara*, Shaw's variations on traditional comic motifs can be sorted out more clearly. A young, often disruptable poet or adventurer wants a young woman or is pursued by her, but some barrier of poverty, birth, or parental disapproval separates them. The fortune both hero and heroine find essential to marital bliss customarily symbolizes a fantasy of power being withheld from them irrationally, it seems, by an aloof but not unsympathetic father figure. This barrier, however, is as much internal as external. For while the preoccupation of Shaw's youthful lovers with sex had led critics to label the plays "prurient," the passion felt by potential spouses is so sharp and impersonal that it hardly survives consummation. Rather, the more lasting, possibly most crippling ties bind son to mother, daughter to father. For example, next to Undershaft's "most dangerous of all infatuations" for Barbara, Cusins describes his own love as a "pale, coy, mistrustful fancy."

Shaw customarily creates his triangles by pairing vital young men with victims of system, those who can and those who can't resist his young heroines' seductive wiles. Nothing so heightens the determination of his rather proper, witty young ladies than resistance from their potential suitors, while nothing so frightens his young men than the single-minded energy of their pursuers. Thus Octavius is paired with Tanner, and Tanner with Don Juan, Blunstschli with Sergius in *Arms and the Man*, Cusins with Steven Undershaft, Randall Utterword with Hector Hushabye, and Captain Shotover with Boss Mangan in *Heartbreak House*. Invariably, a young man's pretensions to vitality are exposed by his willingness to be entrapped, either into marriage or into a sentimental fantasy. His toughest men physically attack father figures, as Brassbound threatens Hallam and Don Juan kills Doña Ana's father. More often, finding words inadequate defenses against women seemingly unmasked as rapacious enemies, they flee into space or withdraw into dreams of power. One mirrors the other, as John Tanner's flight across Europe is juxtaposed with Don Juan's escape to heaven. The disproportion between the rather prim, Victorian moral codes of Shaw's ladies and the fearful resentment they evoke from their "prey" is remarkable, though no less so than his heroines' inability to either keep men worthy of their aspirations happy in marriage or do without men who are not.

The anticomic society with which comedy traditionally begins is symbolized in Shaw by a remarkable proliferation of father figures, sometimes incompetently buffoonish or gentlemanly. Or if powerful, he seems always absent, newly dead, dying, or threatened with death or impotence. Shaw usually portrays such figures at moments when children are about to break into adulthood. To the extent that Caesar, Morell, Undershaft, Ann Whitefield's father, and others demand order and status, fear random drift, and reject mediocrity, Shaw approves, instilling in them a powerful drive to ensure that a new society be continuous with the one it succeeds. Far from acquiescing in any incestuous attachment to his "daughter," he actually assists his younger rival: Caesar promising to send Cleopatra Mark Antony, Tanner being named Ann's guardian, and Blunstschli's father making him fabulously wealthy. In one way or another, Shaw consistently writes what Northrop Frye has called first- or second-phase comedy, in which a young hero is defeated by a humorous society, being assimilated into it or simply running away, leaving it unchanged. Depending on where Shaw places the stress, what looks to the older characters like a fruitful continuation of society's vitality looks to younger ones like the starving of their wilder, livelier virtues—what may happen to Cusins and Hector Hushabye, for instance. The determination with which father-and-son figures are drawn to "compete cooperatively," reducing the heroine to an attractive mannequin, suggests a covert homoerotic pattern with implications of sexual impotence. Almost inevitably, Shaw's father figures quell or divert oedipal feelings away from younger women, often their daughters, at the cost of a heightened drive toward death, experienced by Caesar, Undershaft, Shotover, and others. Moreover, partial or inadequate authority figures complicate efforts to distinguish courage from bluster, intelligence from wiliness. Like the sham kings crowding the battlefield at Shrewsbury in *Henry IV, I*, their proliferation casts doubt on *any* legitimate center of authority. Shaw's keen awareness that impostors abound helps account for his rebelliousness, his championing of democratic freedom, and his denial of outworn claims to legitimacy.

Paralleling the brilliant success of Shaw's young ladies in snaring young men is the dominance of his serene, overpossessive matriarchs over fatherless broods of children. The only husbands present, like Morell in *Candida*, Petkoff in *Arms and the Man*, and Doña Ana's father in "Don Juan in Hell" exercise no more authority than their wives choose to grant them. The others have withdrawn or jealously preserved their bachelorhood, apparently as incapable as their wives or mothers of maintaining any coherent vision of ideality: their "lower" and "higher" passions are as incompatible emotionally as their ideas are logically. As Shaw theorized, those women in his plays who marry choose attractive and virile but mediocre males as biological instruments. Exhausting their husband's potential or driving him away when he resists domination, they create artist-philosophers of their sons, like Henry Higgins (a grown-up Marchbanks), Don Juan or Dubedat in *Doctor's Dilemma*. Not only his artists but his soldiers and businessmen, in their creation and management of fictional empires, manifest their creator's feelings "of rage, jealousy and rivalry, but especially those of helplessness, which rouse a violent, destructive form of aggression against the mother." [8] Reducing men to vessels filled with their meaning, Shaw's women increasingly supplant real but inadequate fathers with idealized equivalents. In *Pygmalion*, Eliza's final apportioning of her body to Freddy and her mind to Higgins crystallizes the temporary, sublimated *ménage à trois* Candida had entered with an older husband and younger poetic outsider; she may imitate Higgins's mother by creating a "marvelous child." In

Heartbreak House, Ellie rejects several inadequate father figures—being asked by Shotover, "What did you expect? A Savior, eh?"—before taking the Captain in a marriage made "in heaven." In *Saint Joan,* the heroine foregoes biological fulfillment altogether, like Ellie, in a version of the Danae myth. Following a suggestion proposed by Lizabeth Sachs and Bernard Stern, Shaw may be projecting upon Joan and God, as his earlier heroines reveal more obliquely, the roles of Mother of Angels and God he imagined for Mrs. Campbell and himself in their impassioned correspondence. In a sense, the apocalyptic moods of *Heartbreak House* and *Saint Joan* culminate in the bombing raid and burning, respectively. These catastrophes divert into apocalypse the suppressed sexual energies of his characters as well as Shaw's own drive to create a vision containing all experience in a single symbol.

Ironically, Shaw's admiration for the passion, tenacity, and vitality of his women is qualified by his distrust of their impersonality, their contempt for abstractions, and their faithlessness. With few exceptions, his heroines remain in flux at the end of his plays, more concerned with fantasies of possessive maternality than with dreams of social progress, despite Barbara's vows and Saint Joan's despair. His great men wrench free of hampering convention to create their own empires, remain ostensibly undistracted by emotion, and seem always to do "the proper thing for the improper reason." But each seems death-obsessed, fearful of sex, insecure, and increasingly disillusioned. It is a measure of Shaw's artistic objectivity that Bentley's formula of "Both/And" should apply with equal fitness to conflicting elements within character as to those within society. However, the balance is an uneasy one, providing the basis of dramatic conflict rather than philosophical integration and harmony, inevitably isolating Shaw from prevailing forces of intellectual ferment.

Heartbreak House (1913–16) is a turning point in Shaw's development as well as the culmination of the drama permeated with discussion he had written in *Getting Married* (1908) and *Misalliance* (1909–10). Shocked and discouraged by the impact of the War upon his evolutionary optimism, Shaw's sense of balance between long-range utopianism and short-range despair has become extremely tenuous. As in *Pygmalion* and *Major Barbara*, he has brought two divided, incomplete families and their hangers-on together as a microcosm of the country's schism; the neurotic insiders are epitomized as the "heartbreakers" and the "equestrian" or governing classes as the "horsebackers." As Fergusson remarks, each person is rather abstract and dreamlike, and each has his own paradoxical pattern to defend and impress upon each of the others. Captain Shotover is fantastically old and wise, and secretly addicted to rum; Ellie Dunn is fresh and virginal, like the Shakespearean heroines she admires, but dedicated to entrapping a rich husband. Critics have noticed the Chekhovian use of ensemble casting, the apparently random and aimless wanderings and discussions, and the heavily charged poetic dialogue. Shaw's characters, however, typically voice awareness of role-playing as Chekhov's would not, though characters in both substitute self-analysis for action.

The impact of Chekhov's *Cherry Orchard* elicited, far more directly than before, Shaw's fantasies of anxiety. The house's nautical fixtures suggest England is a foundering ship, about to drift on the rocks in a war of its own making. The action also projects a kind of shared nightmare of engulfment which is often labeled the Chekhovian myth of fatalism. Shotover's fear of drowning, either literally or in drunken dreams, Mangan's horror of "being buried alive" by hypnotism, and Mangan's swallowing up of Ellie's security echo Chekhov's metaphors of drowning in drink, filth, pointless memories, and futility in *The Cherry Orchard*. Although Shaw takes pains to stress the play's allegorical significance, he retains his focus firmly on the struggles of the individual psyche between the impersonal claims of a corrupt Establishment and a seductive, life-killing fancy.

In an atmosphere charged with threats of dissolution, the "education" of one character by his superior has given way to the ruthless stripping away of masks beneath masks, as in Sartre's *No Exit,* torture "cafeteria style." Following the mode of *Tempest,* we view the forces impelling the house's long-time, middle-aged denizens from the perspective of insiders as one neophyte after another enters its spell. Despair regarding ideals of love, wisdom, and power has sharpened the illusory appeal of fantasies of revelation and rebirth, while living has settled into a matter of repetitive gestures. "I used to writhe under their games at first," Hector confesses, "but I became accustomed to them, and then learned to play them." The play's dynamics reveal a pervasive Sisyphus motif, which later dominates the "Epilogue" to *Saint Joan* involving a haunting anxiety that nothing will ever be done well or permanently. As in *Major Barbara,* the characters' rapid-fire sparring touches on an extraordinary range of literary, social, and political issues, while Shaw focuses on their attempts to disarm and control one another.

Shotover partly represents Shaw, disillusioned, shaken by hostility toward an irresponsible world, and impotent. He is close to Chekhov's old clowns and to Ibsen's failing strong men, Werle, Rosmer, and Solness. His daughter Hesione is marvelously magnetic and attractive, though her fantasy of rescuing Ellie Dunn (the one "real" character in the play) from Boss Mangan is as illusory as Ellie's romance with "Marcus Darnley," her platonic lover. Hector Hushabye is proud and erotic, concealing real courage benath fictional bravado, but trapped in a loveless marriage. Shotover's other daughter, Ariadne Utterword exhibits Hesione's charismatic sexuality. But her grip on respectability kills her spontaneity and invites a shared hypocrisy with others. Ellie's fortune-hunting continues Shaw's earliest reversal of romantic themes, and she sustains the vital otherworldliness appearing in Barbara Undershaft and pressed to its ultimate extreme by St. Joan. Reacting against her father's poverty while idealistically demanding that a husband combine strength with imagination, Ellie is disillusioned with Hector, her Darnley, setting the pattern of education for the following acts. Feeling "quite cured," she turns her attention to Boss Mangan's entrapment.

The second act revolves around Ellie's new-found ability to create workable standoffs between her antagonists and herself. Boss Mangan, who had already provoked Shotover's enmity, is one of the most despicable, selfish, and crude practical businessmen Shaw had ever portrayed in a line going back to Crofts, Burgess, and Lickcheese. Though Ellie fends off his clumsy attempt to destroy her faith in her father and in her own femininity by reducing him to a hypnotized object, he lashes back pathetically, reminding Hesione that "you (Mangan) are a real person: that you had a mother, like anyone else." Disillusioned again by discovering that Mangan's wealth doesn't exist, that he isn't even a "great swindler," Ellie turns to Captain Shotover, only to learn later that his "seventh degree of concentration" is not wisdom, but rum.

At the outset of the third act the characters again assemble, tense and expectant, unable to agree on the source of an ominous drumming in the sky which resembles the snapping string in Chekhov. Preparing for the apocalypse which Shaw had mocked in the brewer Bodger's fiery advertising in *Major Barbara*, Hector had earlier warned, "I tell you, one of two things must happen. Either out of that darkness some new creation will come to supplant us as we have supplanted the animals, or the heavens will fall in thunder and destroy us." But the vision of the superman lies in fragments of which Shotover forms the drifting intelligence, Hector the uninvolved bravery, and Mazzini Dunn the ineffectual idealism. Hovering over the action, personifying those forces who "want to persuade us that we can keep our souls if we let them make slaves of our bodies," in Ellie's words, is the mock-Carlylean figure of Hastings Utterword. Governor of all the crown colonies in succession, he embodies the totally insensitive, totalitarian, and furiously ambitious colonial spirit Shaw had previously treated rather indulgently in Caesar and Undershaft.

By contracting a "spiritual marriage" with Captain Shotover, Ellie rejects previous compromises made by the Shavian heroine. Instead of yoking the actuality of a pliant husband to the vision of a father's spirituality, she seeks "life with a blessing" directly, diverting her frustrated sexuality into hopes for cosmic cataclysm. The drumming in the skies turns out to be approaching bombers, welcomed by the Heartbreakers with lights ablaze. Although the burglar captured in the previous act and Mangan are symbolically blown up while seeking refuge in Shotover's dynamite storage pit, the others are saved. Shaw implies that despite the lateness of the hour and the desperation of our situation, all may yet be well. O'Casey's conclusion of *The Plough and the Stars*, where unrestrained chaos goes far beyond the mental torment of *Heartbreak House*, was unacceptable to Shaw. Yet his characters await the return of the bombers, leaving the alternatives of hope and despair suspended in the void.

Heartbreak House is the turning point of Shaw's career, which is increasingly marked by his tendency to locate his "basis in reality" in "the attitudes of the ironist." In his preface to *Back to Methuselah*, he admits that his powers are waning, and that "the exuberance of 1901 has aged into the garrulity of 1920." Flawed works such as *Too True To Be Good* (1932) and *In Good King Charles' Golden Days* (1939) display enough originality to be considered promising in an unknown playwright, and *The Apple Cart* (1929) and *On The Rocks* (1933) take Shaw for the first time into enactments of behind-the-scenes political manipulation. But a loss of solidity in his settings and social groupings is accompanied by impassioned and unresponsive monologues, one-dimensional characters, and an increasingly hollow optimism.

Whereas *Heartbreak House* dramatizes the impact of a milieu upon a group, *Saint Joan* pits the irresistible force of an obsessed heroine against the immovable objects of social and historical institutions. Bentley finds Joan a synthesis of the practicality of the Lady Ciceleys, the vitality of the Lina Szczepanowskas (*Misalliance*), and the spirituality of the virginal heroines. She also echoes Ibsen's Hedvig in *Wild Duck* and Hilda of *The Master Builder*, ingenues who project crushing burdens of ideality upon fallible father figures. As in Ibsen, the fulfillment of Joan's vision coincides with a spectacular, offstage death scene.

As Shaw has hinted, the play is divided into a romance (scenes 1, 2, 3), a tragedy (scenes 4, 5, 6), and a comedy (the epilogue). In the first three episodes Joan defeats a local baron, overcomes the Dauphin and his assembled court, and then captivates a commander of French forces, apparently aided by miracles, events "which create faith." Rather than evolving, she unfolds. Underlying her native wit, forceful persuasiveness, and love of God is a deep resentment of her own femininity, its dangers and shortcomings. Misunderstood by her earthly father, Joan invokes a unique, obliquely sexualized relationship with a Heavenly Father. Like Hilda Wangel, she views her mind as the womb of time inseminated orally by "voices" through the ear, in a version of Mary's Annunciation. Unwilling to have a flesh-and-blood man either as husband or superior, she attempts to make over both her antagonists and herself into vital, convincingly aggressive men. "I might almost as well have been a man. Pity I wasnt: I should not have bothered you all so much then." She wears men's clothing, bears a phallic sword found mysteriously behind an altar, uses cannon in battle, and is even accused of trying to fly. She fulfills her femininity mythically, however, by identifying her inner turmoil with that of a helpless France impinged upon by father figures: "My father told my brothers to drown me if I would not stay to mind his sheep while France was bleeding to death."

In the clashes between Joan and her antagonists, Shaw divides his sympathies, complicating the inter-action of enlightened individual and reactionary Es-tablishment, female and male. If the array of noblemen and churchmen seem stodgy and out-of-touch, if well-meaning, they are at least reasonable. Joan is viewed as the harbinger of a new era of Protestantism and nationalism, spokesman for intuition and self-fulfillment. But her inner conflicts render her inflexible and, finally, death-centered. Shaw has made Joan's antagonists powerful to stress her pathos, but they are unusually tolerant and articulate, making her progress to the stake depend upon a series of deliberate choices, like those of Antigone.

In the sublot, Joan's impact on Charles the Dauphin is a variation on the Pygmalion motif. He appears initially as a potentially vital character menaced by a malevolent mother and the petrifying burden of his role; puny and easily intimidated though intelligent, he is upset by calls to heroism. As Higgins had turned Eliza from flower girl into mechanical duchess, Joan changes Charles into a king who only looks real, "a dwarf in borrowed robes." Once the crucial vision of "greatness" has been thrust upon him, however, Charles manages the next stage himself. Between Joan's death and the epilogue, he has become bold, athletic, and self-confident, though his sudden terror at the visitation of phantoms is consistent with his earlier appearance.

In the trial scene, Joan's judges struggle to reconcile their humane concerns for her with the pressures of forces they represent. Despite her meteoric rise to prominence, her situation and demeanor are those of a child baffled by its first contact with an adult society. Like Grusha in Brecht's *Caucasian Chalk Circle*, she is tempted, nearly falls, and then reaffirms her original vision, but in Shavian terms. She prefers burning to a living burial which transforms the pastoral peace of the country, once depressingly dull, into fantastically appealing images. By choosing an absurd death, she regains free will, exercising the dominance of male competition she had always desired, though concealed by appeals to traditional values.

In the epilogue, two paradoxes clash—Joan's belief that she was rising above her body to save her spirit and her opponents' views that by destroying her body, they had captured her spirit for society's benefit. Daring as her "resurrection" seems, Shaw found ample models in the revivals of Bottom in *Midsummer Night's Dream* and Falstaff in *Henry IV, I*, to say nothing of innumerable last-minute rescues in Victorian melodrama. The terror with which Joan's antagonists greet her threat to return inverts her attacks on their functions, subtly undercutting the pathos of her final plea: "O God that madest this beautiful earth, when will it be ready to receive Thy saints? How long, O Lord, how long?" In essence, Shaw's own conflict between the creative and rebellious drives of the individual and his need to find satisfying stable roles in society remains in tragicomic suspense.

Among Shaw's contemporaries only Oscar Wilde rivaled his genius without approaching the balance and complexity of his aspirations. While Shaw's drama, unlike his polemics, never failed to confront fantasy with at least the consequences of a rigid, apparently immutable social order, he managed at his best to balance verbal fluency against the perils of futility, the desirable against the attainable.

2

Oscar Wilde

Oscar Wilde's prominence among British dramatists is founded on one masterpiece, *The Importance of Being Earnest* (1895). However, his adoption of a pose of public immorality, the extravagant gestures of a dandy verging on self-parody, and his equation of aesthetic beauty with lying provided him with a public notoriety exceeded only by the sensation of his conviction and imprisonment for homosexuality. As the creator of characters Bernard Shaw publicly stigmatized as "heartless," Wilde was his fellow Irishman's most eminent rival in drama. He was fully content at the same time to accept, even avidly pursue the role Shaw contemptuously tagged "mere entertainer."

Yet Wilde's links with Yeats are perhaps closer. Both support an idealist theatre, characterized not by slice of life imitation of reality but by emotional exhilaration, strangeness, and soaring imagination. "Lying, the telling of beautiful untrue things, is the proper aim of art," [1] Wilde wrote in his aesthetic treatise, *The Decay of Lying,* a book which deeply impressed his countrymen. He and Yeats are both keenly interested in the face behind the mask, the desperate alienation beneath the symbols of societal acceptance and honor. Then too, both are too restless and inventive to accept the restrictions of their highly derivative aesthetic theories. Both writers agree, Richard Ellmann comments, "that art is neither confessional nor photographic, neither wholly subjective nor wholly objective." [2] And Wilde, like Yeats, was a public person, attempting a revitalization of the body politic while maintaining intact, until his sensational disgrace, a hidden and eccentric fantasy world shared with a few like-minded intimates.

Still, society virtually disappears from Yeats's drama as he launches into his most innovative later period, leaving a void between his proud, despairing heroes and a self-sufficient spirit world. For Wilde, however, society is always palpably, demandingly *there*. His plays invert social imperatives, opposing polished surfaces to banal conventions as his society concealed greed, insecurity, and envy beneath polite hypocrisies: all values have become disconcertingly equal—and equally meaningless. Yeats determinedly stares into the abyss of his chaotic unconscious, struggling to hammer his fleeting fantasms into unity. But Wilde uneasily pirouettes, quips, and sings a witty counterpoint against his inchoate strivings, plating over the savage antagonisms of his inner self with decorative postures. As Northrop Frye has said of Shakespeare's, Wilde's comedy holds the mirror up to another mirror and brings resolution out of a double illusion, as reflected in the stylized, balletlike action of his plays.

Wilde's aim as an artist was to reveal art but conceal the maker, commenting that "Art finds her own perfection within, and not outside of herself." However, his inner conflicts, opinions, and lifestyle are transparent in his plays. Wilde's defenses of "the love that dare not speak its name" were usually justified by the excuse that homosexual attachments were extensive among great artists. The "great affection of an elder for a younger man" that "is as pure as it is perfect" [3] is directly portrayed only in A *Woman of No Importance* (1893), where Lord Illingworth is prevented from taking his illegitimate son Gerald for a secretary by the boy's pathetically hateful mother. But the comradely intimacy between such friends as Robert Chiltern and Lord Goring in An *Ideal Husband* (1895) and Jack and

Algernon in *Earnest* reveals a warmth and trust never displayed between Wilde's married couples: "Between men and women . . . there is passion, enmity, worship, love, but no friendship," Lord Darlington tells Lady Windermere. The psychoanalyst Edmund Bergler believes that Wilde's crucial shift from homosexual experimenter to devotee is reflected in *Salomé* (1891) where woman's self-sacrificing kindness disappears and is replaced by "clear-cut cruelty." Unfortunately for Bergler's thesis, none of Wilde's villainous women in his society comedies are quite this flat or simple. Even the vindictive Mrs. Cheveley of *Ideal Husband* has moments of grace. But a noticeable trend does appear.

If not present as a character or attitude, Wilde is there as a dandiacal pose—inverting, mirthfully satirizing, commenting upon a "serious" world, a role Shaw also found congenial. His stress on the artificial, the ordered and the elevated pervades his work in epigrams such as, "Literature always anticipates life. It does not copy it, but moulds it to its purpose." What made him a dramatist, apart from being a poet, novelist, editor, and critic, was his chronic need for love as well as for money. He required constant public reassurance that his fictional metaphors were in fact sensible and not delusory. Wilde had to be reassured that his personal fantasies made him neither grotesque nor ludicrous—"Caliban seeing his own face in a glass"—but loveable, even universally admired.

Although Wilde's social philosphy is as socialistically egalitarian as Shaw's, we get less a theory of social living than a vision of it. His world is polarized between dandy and philistine. He found the types too antipathetic for reconciliation or inner change, ruling out the more complex meshing of vitalist and truly vital character in Shaw. Wilde's image of the affected, ostentatious, and rebellious dandy helps him objectify his feelings and rationalize his art, personifying his aim as a "mask with a manner." On the surface, his resentment is directed at the ascendent bourgeois insistence on realism in art, marriage in sex, incorruptible dullness in politics, conformity in behavior. He supports the creation of a socialistic state which would extend the opportunities for creative individuality from a favored few to the many, freed from the necessities of toil. Yet he never suppresses his sense that uninhibited, transcendent kinds of innovation inevitably arouse the malevolence and envy of society as Nietzsche had warned, fusing them into a punishing mob. He may try to persuade us, like Shaw and O'Casey, that the absurdities of contemporary society can never be mitigated by purifying the individual, only by reshaping the social structure. But even though "what begins as a prank ends as a criticism of life," [4] Eric Bentley concludes, Wilde's dandies remain too rigid and self-sufficient to support any consistent evolutionary drive. In his "pseudo-irresponsible jabbing" at the inconsistencies of an ostensibly Christian culture, attacks he laces with Biblical allusions, he seems more malcontent than rebel. As a social critic, he fills his plays with probing sorties against society, marriage, religion, money, and art; his theorizings are ameliorative, paradoxical, and liberating. But in the depths, he revolts against the fixing of identity (and thus destiny) by anatomy, conditioning, and societal repressions. He longs to withdraw to self-sufficient, idyllic refuges cut off from reality altogether. Thus his existential strivings appear subjective, romantic, and pessimistic.

The conflict between these incompatible modes provides the dialectic of Wilde's plays as it does the humor and detachment typical of his variety of the comedy of manners. By stressing wordplay, gestural brilliance, and formal perfection, all of them essentially preverbal, Wilde "alienates" us; he insulates us from the demands of a conscious world, short-circuiting our repressions. Yet by revealing meaning beneath *non sequiturs*, he strengthens our defenses against the chaos invoked by his aggressive belligerence. By attacking society, he paradoxically reassures us of its solidity and permanence: it is broad and encompassing enough even for rebels and iconoclasts. If society (often personified by demanding matrons) can love us, even after being vilified and subverted, this love therefore means something.

Despite his late-Victorian prominence in writers like Baudelaire, the dandy is not a new character for Wilde and his contemporaries. Nor is it quite accurate to assume that Wilde's society comedies, excepting *Earnest*, are disfigured by the conflict between the dandiacal and the philistine worlds. The complexity of sensation Wilde sought to capture in his art was everywhere frustrated, rather, by the shrinking of his cosmos to a screen-vision of deception and illusion. No suspension of discordant elements in harmony was possible without a vital center sanctioned by myth. And the wider mystery of life was lost for Wilde as surely as it was for Ibsen and Chekhov, as Francis Fergusson has perceived:

> The publicly accepted scene of human life was that of the Philistine bourgeois with its rigid moral and social forms, its sharp blank positivism and the parlor of the carriage trade—and all the rest of human experience illusion.[5]

Wilde's fitful attempts to combine in a single personage a tempter to vice, *raisonneur*, aristocratic poseur, sensualist, and metaphysical clown fail, whereas Shakespeare succeeded in Falstaff. Because an inherited medieval world view was still viable, the world of *Henry IV* was multivalent enough to provide a precariously independent coexistence for the potentially hostile institutions of church, tavern, cloister, innyard, tournament, and court. In the variety of its rituals, Jean Genet's *The Balcony* provides modern drama's closest parallel to Shakespeare. Although the facets of Shakespeare's social cosmos are equally as real as Genet's are unreal, both use civil disturbances to demonstrate the futility of attacks on institutionalized ritual. The rebels in *Henry IV*, like the revolutionaries in *The Balcony*, fail in spite of the impersonations of great figures by usurpers. The impulse to change is subverted by the need to play a role. In Shakespeare, however, the rituals of misrule enacted by Falstaff were designed to consolidate rule, demonstrating the existence of limits by going beyond them.

Wilde was inhibited from either portraying such a ritual and its setting or doing without an emotional safety valve from repressions. His characters seek relief from the coarseness and materialism of a philistine society in escapism, symbolized by Algernon's "Bunburying," a cant term for visiting a male whorehouse, W. H. Auden has told us. Until *Earnest*, Wilde failed to create and sustain a consistent illusion, a world where moral consequences do not exist at all. Only the consequences of believing in a serious world exist. At the end of its action lies a world symbolized by an uncritical, totally accepting power of love, a world which is conventionally labeled "marriage." But the multiple marriages which climax *Earnest* are less an object of belief than an imaginative model of desire opening a new but impossible world for the youthful participants.

Wilde is extremely interested in the status, impact, and function of art, but highly unoriginal in the forms he uses. As a late nineteenth-century British dramatist, he had three potential traditions to tap: the French well-made play, the comedy of manners of Congreve and Sheridan, and the farce of Labiche. After writing a series of melodramatic romances culminating in *Salomé* (1891), Wilde embraced the comedy of manners, filling it with lost children, frantic chases and near escapes, and hidden secrets that farce delights in. His settings are decorative, lushly elaborate versions of the realistic, cluttered drawing room, endowed with the elegant sophistication of country manors, bachelor clubrooms, and lavish townhouses. Although he wrote only four comedies in as many years, he does not really develop. *Earnest* may be the ultimate refinement of a form Wilde seemed fully content with.

As for Wilde's dramatic structure, what invariably happens is that an engaged or married couple find their happiness threatened by an older woman with fewer scruples and more power, as in folklore or romance. After *Lady Windermere*, he pairs the "gay" and "serious" couples of Restoration comedy, making his technical lead more sober and vulnerable than a friend or rival, the dandy-philosopher. Wilde's matron—Mrs. Erlynne, Mrs. Arbuthnot, Mrs. Cheveley, and Lady Bracknell—functions as *architectus*, building up the action onstage, withdrawing from and returning to it, revealing or concealing crucial secrets. She is a symmetrical amalgam of good and evil, power and weakness. Each of them has mysteriously tapped the powers of important but remote male parent figures: Lord Augustus by Mrs. Erlynne, the Church by Mrs. Arbuthnot, Baron Arnheim by Lady Cheveley, and Lord Bracknell by Lady Bracknell. But each matron conceals a sin of greed or lust, however rationalized or sublimated it may seem: desire for control over a husband, child, or prospective relative. Mother and daughter figures are usually paired, sharpening the ambivalence of motives felt by both. As in romance they believe identically that the only choices tolerable for woman are true love, chastity, or death. Thus, Mrs. Erlynne, torn between entrance into society and concealment of her past, risks her daughter's marriage. Mrs. Arbuthnot in *Woman of No Importance* and Mrs. Cheveley face similar dilemmas, risking loss of illegitimate son and potential husband, respectively.

Wilde's emphasis, however, falls on the technical lead, a young man who is to be conducted through a mock ritual of initiation, shown nightmarish visions, and finally granted the symbolic paraphernalia of a secure identity. Lord Windermere's aid of Mrs. Erlynne, Lord Illingworth's illicit affair, Sir Robert Chiltern's betrayal of state secrets, and John Worthing's foundling status all suggest the irrationality of society's requirements for acceptance. Thus, both trivial and significant secrets proliferate in the society comedies. Yet it is remarkable how clumsily, on the one hand, Wilde's heroes conceal their hidden sins, risking their security in return for love, a denial that they are what they have done, as desperately as their antagonists. On the other hand, their antagonists are obsessed with spying into the forbidden, reflecting a cold emptiness in their lives, a lack of willingness to either give or accept affection.

Ironically, the Wildean protagonist encounters identical modes of conduct from ostensible lover and enemy, an assumption that love can only be bought at a terrible price: the fear of its irretrievable loss. The frequency with which a would-be entrapper is trapped by a hand prop—the omnipresent letters, Lady Windermere's fan, Mrs. Cheveley's stolen brooch, the cigarette case, the incriminating mourning clothes, and handbag in *Earnest*—reveals a basic motive force in the comedies. It is as though a protagonist were tempting a punisher, placing unmistakable evidence of wrongdoing in her hands. As a consequence, she must either forgive and forget (as men do, Wilde suggests) or impulsively overreach herself, resulting in public ignominy. Wilde's special wrinkle in the comedies' matched waves of crime and punishment has implications for the war of the sexes. Sir Robert Chiltern complains to his wife in *An Ideal Husband*: "All lives, save loveless lives, true Love should pardon. A man's love is like that. It is wider, larger, more human than a woman's." All Wilde's protagonists actually marry, while devoting a selfless trust primarily to other men. What they desire most deeply is a return to the thoughtless, anxiety-free, emotionally accepted bondage of childhood, as symbolized by the symbiotic union of mother and child: "What this [Mrs. Cheveley] asked of me was nothing compared to what she offered to me," Chiltern pleads. "She offered security, peace, stability." Thus the dandy's marriage in Wilde confirms the temporary triumph of a humorous society over his desires for a fluid, indeterminate, spontaneous existence.

The Importance of Being Earnest achieves a consistency of illusion Wilde's earlier comedies had not attained. Not only have sin and its painful consequences become highly abstract in this remarkably symmetrical play, where every character has a double, a foil, and a partner. But also each psyche is equipped with armor against every impingement, with a line of retreat from every attack—invariably feigned or blunted anyway. As in *Twelfth Night,* no responsible older generation exists, having been replaced by the ridiculous governess Miss Prism, the gullible canon Chasuble, and a foolish aunt, Lady Bracknell. Except for the latter's crucial hold on the fortune of her daughter, Gwendolen Fairfax, the parent figures in the play are totally without authority. All the external barriers to personal and sexual fulfillment have been eliminated in what becomes almost a parody of the state desired by ordinary young lovers. Thus, while the outer action parodies the conventional means by which lost babies, concealed records, misplaced handbags reorder mistaken identities, the inner action involves the removal of inner, psychological barriers to self-realization.

In the first act, Wilde's paired leads, Algernon Moncrieff and Jack Worthing, have devised apparently innocent, childlike fictions to evade the burdens of maturity. Having left his country retreat for town, Jack poses as "Ernest," not only to woo Gwendolen but to escape the "high moral tone" required by guardianship of his ward Cecily Cardew. Algernon's discovery that "Ernest" is fraudulent is complicated by Lady Bracknell's learning he has no right to the name "Worthing" either. Consequently, an ordeal is devised: He must discover a parent or give up Gwendolen. In a play of balanced opposites, the act ends with Algernon's counterstrategy. Having invented a fictional invalid friend Bunbury, designed for the evasion of dull parties and other duties, he will travel to Jack's country place. There, posing as Jack's brother "Ernest," he will woo his ward, Cecily.

The second act moves the action from Algernon's "artificial," male-dominated townhouse to the more "natural," female-controlled country manor owned by Jack. The characters are still further enmeshed in intrigue and misrepresentation. One after another, Algernon arrives as "Ernest," Jack in mourning for the same Ernest's death, and Gwendolen to keep her assignation with Jack. Cecily Cardew is characterized as more fanciful, unspoiled, and flighty than Gwendolen, a "sensible intellectual girl," while Jack must be brought into a true "brotherhood," losing his hostility to flippancy in the process. Ironically, Jack is trapped as farcically by his inappropriate dress as by his lost cigarette case and misplaced identity in the previous act. And when Algernon repeats the counting scene from act 1, he loses the initiative as rapidly as Jack had, never to regain it. They are stripped of their pseudonyms at dizzying speed, thus separating both couples and temporarily uniting the indignant girls as quickly as the boys are estranged.

In their insistence that both young men be named Ernest, the young ladies' fixation is no more startling than the desperation of their suitors' attempts to comply. "A woman married to a man named John would not know the pleasure of a single moment's solitude," Gwendolen had told Worthing, anticipating Cecily's response, "If your name is Algy, I might respect you, but I could not give you my undivided attention." The young ladies seem determined to split off their mates' controllable sobriety, as symbolized by the puns on "Ernest," from their threatening unpredictability and inventiveness. As a result, the men experience sudden but well-founded anxieties that Gwendolen and Cecily will love them not for themselves but for their diverting and theatrical attributes. The only sort of weakness the ladies welcome, apparently, is that attached to readily identifiable stock responses. Thus Cecily astounds Algernon with the scenario of an elaborate, drawn-out courtship ritual, enacted in her fantasy before their meeting, complete with proposal, exchange of rings and letters, quarrel, and reconciliation. None of the youthful lovers is willing to view marriage in terms of genuine, selfless intimacy. "The very essence of romance is uncertainty," Algernon had warned. "If ever I get married, I'll certainly try to forget the fact." Rather than risk rejection and loss of identity, both young men agree to submit to rechristenings. While their "suffering" is a measure of their desire to ingratiate society, it seems disproportionate. Like all the farcical reactions in the play, it serves to cut Wilde's characters off from the "real" world. Yet if the promised rewards of pleasurable sensation are to have proper dramatic impact, he must at least suggest the existence of that world.

In the last act, Lady Bracknell arrives like a comic *diabolus ex machina*, renewing her opposition to Gwendolen's marriage and relenting toward Algernon only when she learns of Cecily's "really solid qualities"—her large fortune. Worthing refuses *his* consent, however, creating an impasse. In the conflicts regarding the men's names and the ladies' fortunes, Wilde has rather audaciously centered all three acts around farcical versions of the Restoration *proviso* scene, set pieces in which couples negotiate their future rights as married persons. However, the deadlock is broken by Jack's identification as Algernon's older brother and Lady Bracknell's nephew. He was the infant victim of Miss Prism's Freudian switch of baby and novel manuscript between bassinette and handbag. His name had been Ernest all along.

The play is technically flawed by leaving Algernon unrenamed and marrying "Jack" to his first cousin. However, with the mass marriage of Chasuble and Prism along with the youthful couples, the play ends in a congenial inclusion of the most disparate personality types typical of the genre. Ironically, a humorous and obsessed society has triumphed over a set of potentially imaginative, rebellious youths. Algernon and Jack are typical of those who lack the will and self-knowledge to either find social confirmation outside their society or to initiate significant reforms.

Both in language and in action the unstable balance between taking or not being taken in emerges in images of food, time, and dissimulation. It is no coincidence that while Algernon indulgently allows his butler Lane to drink as much champagne from his cellars as he wishes, he deprives Lady Bracknell of any cucumber sandwiches, protesting, with Lane's connivance, that there never were any. By giving and withholding oral gratification, he symbolically rewards a "good," un-threatening paternal figure and punishes (trivially) a "bad" maternal one, "eating her up," putting her in-side to end her menace. In act 2, Cecily oversugars Gwendolen's tea and replaces bread and butter with cake, implicitly mocking the "extraordinary sweetness" of her supposed rival's disposition. Plagued with appe-tites as sharp as Algernon's, Gwendolen seemingly links absence of love with hunger, loss of love or hatred with poisoning, establishing malign associations with any-thing she is forced to take in from outside, even includ-ing unpleasant facts. As Jack comments, "the truth isn't the sort of thing one tells to a nice, sweet, refined girl." Thus eating may represent a kind of perception, a be-coming or refusing to become what one contemplates.

Since manipulation of others is such an important value in the play, those who control time are masters, those controlled by it victims. Algernon's ability to take the initiative appears, while it lasts, in his brilliant timing: finishing the sandwiches just before Lady Bracknell's arrival, using the railway timetable to get to Jack's place, appearing just before Jack arrives inappro-priately mourning his "death," lengthening his stay, etc. But man's appetite for love, suggested by Algernon's compulsive eating at fixed times, means he can be baited and trapped, in effect engulfed, by the strait-jacketing marriage ritual. To this extent, Lady Bracknell's marriage portends the futures of the youths. Gwendolen and Cecily will predictably engulf their men, making prisons of their homes and reversing the customary relationships between the sexes. For as a result of having been locked up at home, Lord Bracknell has become not only "quite unknown," but also "painfully effeminate." When it appears their marriages will be delayed until the girls come of age, the men are almost relieved. They still yearn, seemingly, for the timeless world of childhood dreams of irresponsibility. But the girls, sensing their suitors' even greater fears of loss of a fixed identity, cynically torment them by an impatience to wait. While promising never to forget Algernon and Jack, they threaten to marry others soon—and often.

Although only Jack appears literally in disguise, nearly everyone else appears other than what he is. Under their sweet and feminine exteriors, the young ladies are worldly schemers, matching the solid concern for the funds underlying Lady Bracknell's surface silliness. What appears as engulfment of others for the ladies is seen as either "filling" or "protective covering" by the men. Algernon pretends wickedness, but is quickly reduced to conventionality, while Jack has all the instincts and none of the status symbols of the society he so badly wants to enter. Their attempts to deceive and mislead one another by masquerading under false names, inventing exciting offstage roles, and pretending benevolent motives for selfish actions conceal unconscious desires to consume or be consumed, reflecting Wilde's famous jokes linking food with illicit sexuality: "It was like feasting with panthers," as he wrote in *De Profundis*, "the danger was half the excitement." Even love becomes what one puts inside, as Algernon treats food, or puts on outside, like clothing or a rechristening. We sense Wilde's characters are isolated individuals surrounded by incompatible choices, each mode of conduct as farcically incomplete as it is compelling. Marriage serves the same symbolic function in the comedies that death does in *Salomé*. It is a ceremony of exorcism, annihilating irreconcilable discords within one's character. Beneath its finality lies the haunting sense, however, that desires of all kinds—for identity, belonging or lasting love—are beyond the capacity of this life to fulfill them.

Wilde shares with other Irish dramatists a creative mind divided against itself, discernible in an enormous tension between fact and value, reality and appearance. His dandies characteristically adopt one posture after another: assuming false identities, rejecting the claims of conventional morality, fictionalizing their lives, attempting to give their striving meaning at no cost. And moment by moment, as language repeatedly undercuts their situations, we see that all meanings are specious. But since the whole thing is a pretence, involving playful experiments in inauthenticity or invented roles, collapses of identity need have no painful consequences. The fantastic play of wit in Wilde's drama represents the imaginative power of the individual life to continue despite the collapse of social values, a continuing on beyond definition.

Wilde's women, on the other hand, are often cast as moralistic puritans, upholding some institutional standard of virtue as harsh and immutable as it is egalitarian and impersonal. Lady Windermere, Mrs. Arbuthnot, and Hester Worsley in Woman, both Mrs. Cheveley and Lady Chiltern in Ideal Husband, and Lady Bracknell assume that one plays one's part in society as though it were divinely ordained. If each man is not his name and does not play the role his name implies—statesman, husband, father, guardian—he must be compelled to do so or be punished by loss of love and respect. Symbols of identity should be absolutes, they feel; names of personal qualities should be transcendently effective regardless of personal volition, despite male protests that "public" and "private" lives are different things. "They have different laws and move on different lines," in Chiltern's words. However, their need for love is so great, despite its terrible cost, that Wilde's men conform to values they intuitively feel are false. By taking on fictional identities, they symbolize their wish to escape from the body with which they are recurrently and inevitably left when identity has collapsed.

It is ironic that Wilde's extraordinary drive to master his inner conflicts destroyed him in real life. W. H. Auden suspects that

> His secret day-dream [at his trial] was of a verdict of guilty being brought in whereupon Judge, jury and public would rise to their feet, crown him with flowers and say: "We ought, of course, to send you to gaol, Mr. Wilde, but we all love you so much that in this case we are delighted to make an exception." [6]

Nothing of the kind, as we know, happened. Yet it is more important that Wilde's energies resulted, after several flawed attempts, in the culminating mastery of *The Importance of Being Earnest*.

3

W. B. Yeats

Among the great modern Irish dramatists, W. B. Yeats may be the most enigmatic—at once open and concealed, both simple and complex. His poetic preeminence is undisputed, at least among writers in English. Yet his plays have dropped from the repertory of the Abbey and may even be unproduceable today. The considerable authority of his accomplishment in the drama is undeniable, though, for his sensitive and perceptive peers. For all the social and ideological conservatism of his plays, their peculiar vibrancy and spontaneity reflects Yeat's enormous resources of imagination. Despite his leadership of nationalist agitations, his aristocratic prejudices, and his refusal to accompany many of his artistic countrymen into exile, Yeats is an extremely ambivalent artist. His works, for all his elitist tendencies, remain almost embarrassingly rooted in the sweat and mire of desperate human struggle.

Superficially, J. M. Synge seems Yeats's closest associate in his revival of revitalized Irish poetic theatre. Both reject a theatre of protest, ideology, and persuasion, an approach Yeats took only fleetingly in his early *Countess Cathleen* (1892) and *Cathleen Ni Houlihan* (1902). If their countrymen are to be saved, it will come not through the reform or destruction of institutions, but through a rebirth of humane sensitivity. Both are absorbed by the artless, "poetic" speech patterns of an untutored peasantry, free of stultified, materialistic reflexes. And although both attempted, for a time, to reveal the temper of their nation through realistic treatments of folkloric incidents often in remote, unblemished settings, both involuntarily overcame the narrow theoretical limitations they imposed on their art.

Still, for all their resemblances Yeats is even further removed from Synge than Shaw is from Ibsen. Rather than letting his stories spread outward toward other stories without, however, losing their roots in psychological states of mind as Synge and O'Casey did, Yeats deliberately used mythic patterns in the mode of Eliot and Joyce; he pulled them in or brought them down to earth in concrete, modern meanings. Synge's awareness of evil exists side by side with a very strong sense of personal identity. His fury at inhumanity is mollified by his personal warmth and social optimism. But for Yeats, the personality is split apart and acknowledged to be so. He is harrowed by a sense of inner pulsations between fixed, dangerously inadequate and unstable poles. Synge's concretely sensuous language both links and distances his characters' passion and contemplation. Yeats's personae, like Pirandello's, are created and seen to be masklike, stripped down to their abstract humanity. Bereft of a self in its health and complexity to mitigate their sense of panic and emptiness, they see no refuge from unceasing inner conflict in their blinding rationality.

Yeats is probably one of the most subjective writers in modern British drama, producing autobiographical plays on a scale far beyond O'Casey. His hopes of captivating Maud Gonne constantly reappear in this early drama, where his persona Aleel fails to dissuade the Countess Cathleen from selling her soul for the starving Irish peasantry. And in *The Shadowy Waters* (1911) the warrior-bard Forgael kills Dectora's husband, enthralls her with his harp, and drifts off into the misty distance with her. Then too, his mingled admiration and resentment of his articulate father appear not only in his treatments of the Cuchulain myth, which overlay the ritual of the dying and reviving nature god, but in his characters' recurring oedipal crises. The great literature of the past, the oral legends of the Irish peasantry, and the occult correspondences of the mystic societies he joined all supplied a body of symbolism from which the poet constructs a mask. Forever trying to catch the elusive essence of the universe and fix it with an image, Yeats wrote, echoing Wilde, "I have often had the fancy that there is some one myth for every man, which, if we but knew it, would make us understand all he did and thought." [1] Believing that Irish writers must "dig our furrows with the sword," Yeats called for a "theatre of speech, of romance, of extravagance." He adjusted to Synge's shift from mysticism to peasant naturalism with some difficulty, was a notoriously inept director of Abbey actors, and severely crimped both the Abbey and O'Casey's development by his misguided attacks on naturalism in the 1928 *Silver Tassie* controversy. Refusing like Henry James to leave a theatre where he was misunderstood and ignored, he reveals some of the bitterness he felt in the speech of a choral figure introducing *The Death of Cuchulain*. After demanding a small and elite audience steeped in the classics, he protests, "If there are more than a hundred, I won't be able to escape people who are educating themselves out of the Book Societies and the like, sciolists [smatterers] all, pickpockets and opinionated bitches." Despite the personal egotism and self-satisfaction of Yeats's manifestoes and defenses, he is a stern and rigorous ironist in his plays. Although aside from Milton's *Comus,* he is the only playwright alluded to by his characters, they usually comment on his obscurity. In *The Player Queen* (1915), the Prime Minister much prefers his farcical *Noah* to the players' choice of "some dull poetical thing, full of long speeches," and one sitter in *Words on the Window Pane* (1934) likens the spirits of Swift and Vanessa to "characters in some kind of horrible play."

Unlike Shaw's drama of ideas or Wilde's drama of wit, Yeats composed a drama of images. Personally optimistic, his dramatic theory was directed until the Easter Uprising at showing the country's "young men images for the affections, though they be but diagrams of what it should be or may be." But after 1916, Yeats became more interested in the poetic drama as a means of coping with the divided, shifting perspective of his insights. As his social pessimism deepened, his faith in salvation through political action diminished. In the thirties he finally rejected all forms of government with some asperity: "Republics, Kingdoms, Societies, Corporate States, Parliaments, are trash, as Hugo said of something else, 'not worth one blade of grass that God gives for the nest of the linnet.'" Rather, maintaining at one and the same time the beliefs that the creator finds his own artistic symbolism and that the truth behind his scheme is a spiritual illumination, he focused on the validity of his art for contemplation, not for practical utility. Yet like Shaw, he continues to create plays in which plot and character are largely subordinate to theme; and both lean toward the heavy use of extradramatic material in their plays: Shaw's discussions and Yeats's song, dance, and masks.

As for Yeats's dramatic structure, it was both derivative and unpopular with his potential audiences until he neared the end of his career, when his practice began to diverge from his theory. His action is nearly always rigorously focused, tying and then untying a dramatic knot, as Ronald Peacock observes.[2] Terms like "remote, spiritual and ideal" appear in his early attacks on naturalism, and later, "distinguished, indirect, symbolic." He relies on a private and intimate tone, traditional symbolism, aristocratic nostalgia, and a bare or sketchily decorated stage. As in O'Casey, his plays' initial tension arises from his characters' fear of impingement or violation. Drawn back to some place where they had experienced a traumatic incident, they sense a menace lurking beyond fragile boundaries—some betrayer with unknown intentions or supernatural powers, or both. The crisis of the play, "tying the knot," is brought on by the forced entrance of an antagonist making some intolerable yet irresistible demand. Like the characters of Pirandello, Yeats's try to accommodate the attractions of opposite forms of existence—face and mask, formal perfection and ecstatic energy—at the same time. Consequently, paralysis brings on sudden, dramatic seizures, "untying the knot," so unlike the gradual recognitions attained by Eliot's characters. Yeats's language evolved with his dramatic modes, moving from an early, lyric indefiniteness to a harder, masculine realism. Near the end, he experimented successfully with prose interspersed with lyrics, a sparely unpoetic diction, and an essentially synthetic speech unifying the demands of action and contemplation.

Yeats's drama, then, is a compressed psychodrama of compulsion, presenting an irreconcilable conflict between transformation and identity, time and immutability. The basic Yeatsian action is dialectical, subject to innumerable combinations and permutations. He accepted and even eagerly courted change as an escape from sterile and constricting forms. But he also recognized how vulnerable and painfully exposed he became, not only to the egoistic demands of others, but to the ravages of his own unleashed anxieties. If the mask sometimes freezes up his sources of inspiration, aggravating his aloof shyness from other social beings, it is more often his last refuge of inner security. The figures of Lazarus and Judas both betray Christ in *Calvary*, personifying the opposing motives implicit in the Yeatsian extremes. Envious of a Christ who "travels toward the death I am denied," Lazarus feels exposed and threatened; he wishes only to return to his warm, womblike tomb. Judas, on the other hand, found his identity drowned in God's power. Acting on his belief that "whatever man betrays him will be free," he destroyed Christ's selfhood to preserve his own. Only he discovered that his own identity—that of a traitor—was equally intolerable: "now you cannot even save me." All Yeats's characters grapple with the problem of reconciling individual freedom and creativity with the values of society, seen to be both narrow and overpowering.

Since almost all of Yeats's characters are aspects of his divided self, they can be roughly divided into two types: active and passive, those who attempt to impose their fantasies upon others and those who are transformed by a vision from some immanent source. But whether dynamic or accepting, almost all of Yeats's characters associate the instincts with a terrifying sexuality. In his rather obscure and mystical volume, *A Vision*, Yeats constructs an elaborate system of recurring and alternating personal, historical, and cosmic cycles of development. His pattern of whirling, interpenetrating cones or "gyres," which he felt represented the archetypal pattern of all life, was most strikingly duplicated by the unity of man and woman in intercourse. With the possible exception of Tennessee Williams, no other playwright of Yeats's stature has hinged so many dramatic crises on a single act of intercourse. Nor until Genet has one dealt in such detail with copulation on the stage. Invariably, sex is identified with respite from battle, followed by loss, "a kiss / In the mid-battle, and a difficult truce / Of oil and water, . . . a brief forgiveness between opposites," as Cuchulain describes it in *On Baile's Strand*. For Yeats, physical satisfaction leads directly to disaster, symbolized by the recurrent beheadings (representing castration) which befall Cuchulain, the swineherd of *Full Moon in March*, and others. Not only sex but passions of any uncontrollable kind are seen as a source of danger to Yeats: anger, revenge, betrayal are all vital elements in his work, and all stand condemned. No matter how powerfully his protagonist's urge for perfection drives him upward, toward some permanent and imperishable receptacle of the spirit, his restless and aggressive instincts draw him downward into self-absorption, fruitless passion, the dark.

Yeats is probably trying to come to terms with these

emotions in himself, for when his persona feels exposed to intolerable demands or beset by hostility, he yearns to construct a golden labyrinth of the mind. He seeks to

> build in his free consciousness buildings vaster and more sumptuous than those built by science, furnished too with all manner of winding passages and closets and boudoirs and encircled with gardens well shaded and with everything else he can desire.[3]

As in *Resurrection,* where the disbelieving Greek discovers "The heart of a phantom is beating!" within the side of the resurrected Christ, Swift tells Vanessa in *Words,* "When I rebuilt Rome in your mind, it was as though I walked its streets." The presence of a living voice, spirit, or beating heart within a golden artifact, phantom, severed head, or medium duplicates in art Yeats's "burning mask." As spirit enters frame, Yeats fantasizes his own entrance into the minds of a captivated audience through the words of his plays, it could be speculated. Whatever form it takes, Yeats's desire for ideality and permanence reflects his need to escape the feared deterioration of the body and its beauty, to fulfill his wish for a self-replenishing immortality.

Yet since concepts are the death of spontaneity, even the idealized refuge may become a prison house of emptiness and desolation. Assailed from within by an uncontrollable hunger and thirst for sensation, his protagonists are often tormented by unremitting observation by some sort of "evil eye," their own blinding rationality turned inward. The plight of characters isolated both from themselves and their worlds, is graphically depicted in Yeats's first published play, *Countess Cathleen.* When the starving peasants attempt to sell their souls for gold, a pair of bargaining demons "magically" detect cracks in their souls. Next to the anxieties of sexuality, the pangs of hunger and thirst recur through his plays, reflecting his desire to take in the world's freshness and sensations, often through the eyes. Yet he feels so fragile that he fears real intimacy will pierce and eviscerate him, the fate of Dionysus.

For Yeats's protagonists, then, an idealized model may serve as an instrument for securing the subjection of others not to him, but to it. In *The King's Threshold*, for example, the poet Seanchean is slowly starving himself to death to force King Guaire to restore an ancient prerogative called "The Poet's Right." As one after another pupils, public officials, princesses, and his fiancée implore him to accept substitutes, he rebuffs them. Deliberately straining the social fabric by endangering the king's authority, he hopes to extract from his society, in an atmosphere of rebellion, their total submission. This gesture, he affirms through his dramatically effective act of self-denial, is due not to himself alone (he pretends), but solely to his rank and function as a poet. But he is not so much interested in the kind of honor that can be had in his society as he is anxious to place himself beyond all possible honors, to have himself recognized as an absolute no mere king—let alone lesser mortals—can judge. In their frenzied efforts to achieve this recognition, Yeats's Cuchulain, his Swift, his swineherd, and numerous other protagonists feign resignation as they rush toward self-destruction. On the surface, Yeats rejects the mediocre art, the social hypocrisies, and the political injustice of contemporary bourgeois society; in the depths he seeks escape from the helplessness of will and the anxieties of intimacy. Socially, he is objective, inspirational, realistic, and Establishment; but existentially, he is subjective, passive, romantic, and pessimistic, a part of the consciousness of an age which cannot be understood without him, as T. S. Eliot has remarked.

Although Yeats's production amounted to over twenty-five separate plays composed over a period of half a century, from 1884 to 1939, he was an evolving rather than an unfolding writer, a fact which must have dismayed him occasionally. At the beginning of his apprenticeship, Yeats reacted against the claptrap of

Victorian melodrama and the newer naturalism which was replacing it as firmly as O'Casey later embraced them. Instead, he turned out a series of rather misty, escapist pre-Raphaelite plays based on Irish folklore. Then, coinciding with his indefatigable work with Lady Gregory in founding the Abbey Theatre in 1904, he modeled a series of peasant farces on those of Synge and Lady Gregory.

The Player Queen is Yeats's first successful play. After struggling to write it as a tragedy for nearly eight years, he quickly finished it (at Pound's suggestion) as a farce in 1915. It is composed in two scenes or interlocking panels. The first deals with the efforts of a poet named Septimus both to punish himself for loving a cruelly beautiful wife, and to restrain an angry crowd from attacking the palace of the never-seen Queen, whom they believe is a witch. In a second scene, inside the palace, the country's harried Prime Minister tries to prepare his countrymen for the dual coronation and marriage of the Queen (to himself) by staging the farcical Chester *Noah* Play.

Aside from the offstage Dionysus-worshippers in *The Resurrection* (1931), the first-scene crowd of rebellious citizens and countrymen is Yeats's last use of a microcosmic social group. Although the Irish rhythms of their speech are faulty, the play's prose marks a decisive break with his past lyricism. And like the mobs of Shaw, Synge, and O'Casey, their emotionality swings between predictable extremes. Either they grovel in worshipful abasement before an idol of impossible desire, "a holy woman" who "prays for us all"; or should someone else seem to be in possession, as the fanciful report of her "coupling with a great white unicorn" suggests, they react with bitter anger and brutality, confusing devotion to chastity with an act of lust. The appearance of a crazed old donkey-man who rolls in straw and brays to signal a change of crown foreshadows the second-scene denouement. Along with the bad popular poets who had appeared earlier, the *Vates* neatly brackets Septimus as impractical poet of genius.

The second scene, which drives toward the substitution of the queenly actress Decima for the unwomanly Queen, combines an outer romantic plot with an inner plot of development, the disillusioning of Decima. Between them both stands Nona, Septimus's practical, commonplace mistress and Decima's rival. Ironically, the conflicts embroiling the mismatched and interlocked love triangles proceed with the stately refinement and orderly exchange of partners typical of dance. As the two images of the Queen, nun and witch, circle the perplexed Prime Minister (in fantasy), Decima and Nona circle Septimus until a crisis separates them. When she discovers that Septimus's love poetry had been written in bed with Nona, Decima disdainfully throws her rival both dramatic part and husband. She then announces her intention to "choose a new man" from the players dressed in animal costumes as they dance around her. With the arrival of news of the mounting fury of the mob, a frenzied space of circular movement occurs, each one pursuing and pursued, followed by a cross-movement. Wishing to die in the Queen's golden gown and slippers, Decima circles briefly with the Queen, who then withdraws to merge with her idealized image of the martyred St. Octema. Decima then merges with the image of queenliness and circles with the Prime Minister. Leaving Nona with Septimus, she gains the stability and permanence she had wanted all along. In his most Shavian play, Yeats has fused the multiple implications of the play by interpenetrating the modes of dance, farce, and discussion.

Decima's education forms the inner action of the play, teaching her that freedom depends largely on the destruction of self-erected barriers. At the beginning she had been as much used for Septimus's poetic purposes as he had been abused by her erratic disdain. The death of the old and rebirth of the new Decima proceeds through her emergence from the womblike throne, taking food and drink from Nona, and changing clothes with the Queen after her narrow escape from suicide. In a parody of the Pygmalion motif, the Prime Minister fails to turn an inept Queen into a mechanical doll, but unknowingly makes a doll-like actress into a real woman, a Queen for whom regal gestures are an adequate substitute for royal birth. Although both Septimus and the Prime Minister serve as catalysts, changing without being changed, Decima creates a new woman from her platonic image of herself. Yet her character remains very much in flux at the end of the play. Her description of her discarded self as "a bad, headstrong, cruel woman" who "seeks destruction somewhere and with someone she knows nothing of" sounds like some kind of principle. The only moral seems to be that each character should act according to the law of his own nature. In Septimus's words, "Man is nothing till he is united to an image."

While completing *The Player Queen*, Yeats discovered through Pound the Noh play of Japan, which was as congenial to his own dramatic talents as it was strange to his contemporaries. In five plays written in as many years, he adapted incidents from the Cuchulain myth, Irish folklore, and Christian legend to the convention of a priest's visit to a shrine. There, he has a vision of an episode connected with the place. As in his source, the imagery of plays such as *At the Hawk's Well* (1915) and *Calvary* (1920) is concrete and sensuous, real and phantom worlds coexist, and both staging and acting are ritualistic and abstract.

After giving up the theatre for a time, Yeats began creating after 1926 his last, most innovative plays. In works such as *The Words Upon the Window Pane* (1930) and *The Herne's Egg* (1938), his protagonists are rootless, passionate old men, raging at the disparity between ebbing vigor and keen sexual desires. Through an imaginative use of the Elizabethan "play within a play" convention, Yeats asserted the superiority of fantasy over sensate reality, obsession to routine, while stressing sharply the "primal scene" aspects of the device: its roots in fantasies of parents engaged in intercourse. As in dream, violent and painful actions are committed abstractly by personified wills, usually in gamelike situations. Sudden transformations of essences into their opposites, or the unification of antitheses through paradox, occur. Thematic interests previously implicit in his drama become more prominent: the sadomasochistic battle of the sexes; a growing horror of apocalyptic cataclysm; the yawning gap between spiritual aspirations and brute will to power; an encroaching nightmare of senseless, recurrent pain, equating an easeful death with pleasure. As rapacious fantasies are more readily enacted, dialogue becomes interiorized, replacing responsive speech with interrupted monologues.

Having destroyed reality in his Noh Plays for Dancers, Yeats attacked stage reality itself in *Words*. A motley group of Irish spiritualists have gathered for a furtive seance with an imported medium, Mrs. Henderson. The lodging house in which they have rented a room is a fit symbol of both Jonathan Swift and his era, being decayed and yet full of memories like the inscription from a poem of Stella's cut into one of its windows. Yet the setting is shrunken and myopic by comparison with the bustling throne rooms of *On Baile's Strand* and *The Player Queen*. Unlike the isolated natural locales of *At the Hawk's Well* or *The Herne's Egg*, it is surrounded by an urban wasteland. In his counter-Ibsenite tragicomedy of revelation, Yeats has used the devices of the naturalistic theatre to subtly undercut its assumptions about the knowability of reality. His characters form a social microcosm, but with no religious, social, or patriotic assumptions in common. Only curiosity, greed, or loneliness temporarily unite them. Among the stock types or "humour" characters, a young scholar named John Corbet, writing a thesis on the age of Swift, functions as Yeatsian *raisonneur*. Since he is well informed historically, though a skeptical novice regarding spiritualism, his enlightenment by and of the other characters supplies most of the play's exposition.

Before the session begins, the society's president, Dr. Trench, quells an effort to exorcize spirits who have spoiled previous seances in the room, explaining that they relive a passionate moment of life until purged of remorse. As the sitters form a sort of uncomprehending but expectant chorus, almost a dance figure, by holding hands, the spirits of Swift and Vanessa again intrude, speaking through Mrs. Henderson's lips. In an ironic courtship game, Vanessa presses Swift to accept marriage and procreation. More eloquently, Swift objects to Vanessa's inquisitive prying; he also fears a child might inherit his own incipient madness or, even if healthy, "add another" to the "knavery of the world." Beneath his hope that by educating Vanessa he might enter the rebuilt Rome he had made of her mind, lies the displacement of her womb upward, where it is identified with her mind, a defense against fearful sexual anxieties.

To Vanessa, however, Swift's subtle rationale is nonsense. Uncomplicated, healthy in her judgments, and concrete in her thinking, she immediately spots the inauthenticity of those who find the desires of ordinary mortals distasteful: "Jonathan, Jonathan, I am a woman, the women Brutus and Cato loved were not different." Vanessa functions in the inner action as Corbet does in the outer one, as Jamesian *ficelle* eliciting Swift's contradictory aspirations: his desires for both the admiration of great colleagues and withdrawal to an idealized past, being worshiped as a near-deity or loved as a fallible man. Paradoxically, the natural force that draws Vanessa toward Swift is possible to the extent that she remains free of his concern for posterity, that she finds emotions meaningful in and of themselves: "You said you have strong passions; that is true, Jonathan—no man in Ireland is so passionate. That is why you need me, that is why you need children, nobody has greater need." Her natural spontaneity, the source of her love for Swift, is preserved by her freedom from what people think, her resistance to thinking "as Cato or Brutus would," the masks of Swift.

During a hymn-singing, Stella replaces Vanessa as

Decima had replaced the Queen, a version of the recurrent Yeatsian exchange trick he had used as early as *The Shadowy Waters* (1911). Swift's anticipation that "You will close my eyes, Stella" not only personifies her as an easeful, eroticized death, but glances at his desire for freedom from his guilt-provoking wishes "to see into," displaced on Vanessa's mind. Despite the failure of the seance, the sitters make a ceremony of paying the medium. Preferring fantasies to real, spontaneous intimacy, they resent calls to rebirth as bitterly as Swift does. Instead, looking to Fate for some assurance beyond that provided by society, they hope a graceful acceptance of loss may yet ingratiate potentially hostile spirits.

The play ends, then, in loss and lack of vision. The scholar Corbet fails to see the sterile and contradictory forces lashing Swift's era, vitiating his optimistic and comfortable thesis. Having gained no release in death from his lacerating, savage indignation, Swift emerges as a victim. His appearance near the end of life and play parodies the concept of normal, spontaneous fruition: "Some disease had made one of his eyes swell up, it stood out from his face like a hen's egg." As she wanders aimlessly around the kitchen, Mrs. Henderson is again subject to a seizure by Swift's agonizing spirit, ending the play with Job's despairing words: "Perish the day on which I was born!" By restoring the perspective of routine, uncomprehending human existence at the end, Yeats makes the spirits appearing in the seance more tangible while rendering the persons of the sitters more ghostly by contrast, giving the play the dramatic impact of a double exposure. At the end, the society of the play, ours as well as Swift's, simply vanishes with the sensation of an awakening from nightmare, dissolving not into some refuge of the purified soul but into nothing.

Yeat's attack on stage reality is extended to the ultimate in the ironically named *Purgatory* (1938), possibly the most compressed and perfect of all his dramas. Although he uses the conventions of the Noh, returning his aged antihero to his burned-out birthplace to liberate his mother's ghost from purgatorial torment, Yeats is too subjective, too idealist to allow the action simply to unfold. By the time he wrote the play, he realized that his hopes for the synthesis of present and past, art and politics, were futile. In portraying an Old Man's invocation of the scene of his own conception, the murder of his son, and the consequent failure of his exorcism of his parents' ghosts, Yeats focuses on the dynamics of elemental family relationships to the exclusion of character.

His use of the "play within a play" convention to depict a son seeing his father in the role of lover, a "primal scene," paradoxically attacks a theatre audience's desire for the representation of reality by literally gratifying the voyeurism they share, presumably, with the author. As in *Words*, he makes the inner action "historical," the outer action "philosophical," in Pirandello's terms, though both are equally products of his imagination. But by detailing the son's education from skepticism to horrified belief, Yeats creates the illusion that the Old Man is as subject to the "historical" vision of his past as the spectator is. And although he goes even further than Pirandello in breaking down the barriers between the inner and outer plays, he uses the convention for the same purposes as the Elizabethans and his Italian contemporaries. Since the Old Man lives in two worlds, both his world of illusion and a world of reality, he combines the roles of visionary, actor, and chorus—commenting, expostulating, and criticizing. Thus, far from destroying illusions, Yeats actually multiplies them.

The fire-ruined shell of a house and the lightning-riven tree which dominate the set objectify thematic splits between an aristocratic, "maternal" past and a brutalized and fallen "paternal" present. While the house's burning by the Old Man's drunken father, whom the Old Man killed at the time, may represent the killing of a nation, family, or even individual, the tree may symbolize the multiple conditions of life, senescence, and death of the human soul. And the play's moonlit darkness, the characters' comings and goings to and from nowhere, and the haunted demeanor of the Old Man heighten the dreamlike mode of the play. The Old Man resembles Shakespeare's King Lear in his intense, limited passion, his isolation in an alien universe, and his ambivalence toward his progeny. But Shakespeare's historical and natural dimensions are missing. Beneath the play's most literal level of conflict, whether the Old Man's vision is "out there" or only a distorted image in his maddened brain, is his insistence on purgation, if not of his mother, then of himself. Irrevocably split between his mother's refinement and his father's coarseness, he has found learning, storytelling, fornication, and wandering inadequate strategies for living in an intolerable situation. In returning to a scene he could not possibly have witnessed, he may wish to restore—in the moment of conception—the only togetherness of mother, father, and child that life ever affords. Underlying his deep-seated guilt feelings as to his mother's death in childbirth are the Old Man's terrible preoccupation with balancing off love and hate, separating the guilty "not-me" from the innocent "me."

This dualism extends to the structure of the play: two waves, one of crime, one of punishment. His futile repetition of doing and undoing also groups the play's offstage characters. Aligned with the three men, fathers and sons all, are three incomplete maternal figures: the Old Man's punishing grandmother; his sensitive yet lustful mother; and the mother of his own son, still linked with the ditch of his conception. All these fragmented wills reflect the Old Man's insuperable problem of separating the idealized spirit of his mother from her befouled body. Should she be imagined as a golden labyrinth, whom he might love as men "had loved the house, had loved all / The intricate passages of the house," or is she like its darkened shell, a sulphurous trap?

Since the Old Man exalts "art" above "life," he also

wants the fatherhood of authorship, linking him with his creator at the locus of the primal scene:

> Go fetch Tertullian; he and I
> Will ravel all that problem out
> Whilst those two lie upon the mattress
> Begetting me.

By killing his son, who is drawn into the same state of revengeful greed by his shared vision, he not only punishes his own sexual desires retrospectively, but stops (he thinks) an endless chain of guilt and retribution. Yet no solution is reached; he hears the beat of his father's hoofbeats again and finds himself "Twice a murderer and all for nothing." The only solution he had left, to keep talking to drown the fantasies that threatened his existence, is vitiated. As in *Deirdre, On Baile's Strand*, and *Words*, father "kills" son, past destroys the future. The ultimate tension which racks the Old Man in *Purgatory* is the tension between his unshareable vision and his need for love, what is and what he had wished to make of it.

Together, Old Man and son balance the dual aspects of Yeats's divided self, but with a great deal more subtlety than he may have fully realized. The Old Man's love of the past, his insistence on spiritual vindication, and his fascination with a deathly sexuality are all qualities found in his early Cuchulain and Christ alike; these are now exposed as attitudinizing with more than a touch of self-pity and morbidity. And the son's concern for a life of the senses, the here and now, represents the skeptical, impatiently objective impulse in Yeats turned back upon itself, reflecting a great uneasiness with his own and his age's intolerance of imaginative transformation of the spirit.

Yeat's dramatic career ends without any resolution of the contradictory aspirations he had experienced all his life. His protagonists, Swift, Cuchulain, King Congal, all aspire towards the cauldron of destructive passions, hoping to rise from the bondage of the flesh toward renewed spiritual life. But each is fated to plunge downward within the cycle of nature, caught within its demonic repetitions of humiliation, despair, and extinction. Just as the spirit of the swineherd in *Full Moon* cannot join the stars without prior desecration, in the parodic tragedy *The Herne's Egg*, King Congal is literally reborn as a donkey after dying at the hands of a fool, his own. The natural cycle which contains each of them is usually symbolized by an ambivalent female figure, part virgin and part harlot, whose ambiguities Yeats never resolved. His desire for an aristocracy of the spirit emerged near the end in some unattractive flirtations with fascism, but his hope for an ideal art remains untainted by simplistic formulas. Only by accepting his opposing selves, mask and creator, could he continue to function with artistic sensitivity. His drama remains the final measure of this aspect of his genius, his continued willingness to make art of his quarrels with himself.

4

J. M. Synge

J. M. Synge quickly earned the status of resident genius of the Abbey Theatre during his brief career (1902–1909). But in many ways he was an anomaly in Irish literature and modern drama. His reputation on the Continent grew with productions in Paris, Prague, and Berlin during his lifetime, while Irish audiences greeted his plays in Dublin with riots and ridicule so abusive that one of them, *The Tinker's Wedding*, was not performed there in his lifetime. Despite his admiration, Yeats admitted himself unable to duplicate the earthy, colorful speech rhythms of the Irish peasantry, whose dialect has assimilated a seventeenth-century idiom within Gaelic syntax. Beneath the surface of Synge's picturesque language lie depths of despair, Rabelaisian sensuality, and sardonic bitterness; between the surface and Synge's deeper concerns there is a constant ironic tension. Contradictions between the man himself and Yeats's phrases such as "passionate and simple" seemed resolved only by his early death.

As a member of the middle-class Protestant Ascendancy, descended from a family rich in bishops and landowning aristocracy, Synge earned a university degree, studied music in Germany, and read literature in the Sorbonne. To Yeats's occasional exasperation, he had no politics, religious ties, or strong national loyalties; he shrank from the crucible of commitment as resolutely as Yeats sought out, even created it. An antiquarian rather than a revivalist, he viewed himself as an Irish European seeking the roots of creativity in the imagination of the people. Yet at the very end of his life he was thinking of abandoning his remote and picturesque settings, anecdotal fictions, and recognizable characters. In their place he was considering highly experimental, absurdist conceptions which would have severed his collaboration with the Abbey as surely as Yeats's and O'Casey's experiments did. For a writer of his stature, Synge's production was quite slight. *In The Shadow of the Glen* (1903) and *Riders to the Sea* (1904) are short, and *The Tinker's Wedding* (1907) is medium length; *The Well of the Saints* (1905), *The Playboy of the Western World* (1907), and the unfinished *Deirdre of the Sorrows* (first performed 1910) are full length.

As an intellectual, a protestant, and an artist, Synge took an equivocal view of the Irish peasant and his milieu. Aloof and objective, he prided himself on capturing the unalloyed essence of his subjects' speech. His art was best advanced, he felt, by the Elizabethan collaboration between dramatist and his social group. He depicts himself as not only impersonal but invisible in his much-maligned eavesdropping reference, meant to establish the validity of his characters' speech:

> When I was writing "The Shadow of the Glen," some years ago, I got more aid than any learning could have given me from a chink in the floor of the old Wicklow house where I was staying, that let me hear what was being said by the servant girls in the kitchen.[1]

His resistance to the "joyless and pallid words" of Ibsen and Zola stemmed more from the didacticism he thought he detected in their works than from their reliance on prose, to which Eliot objected. So rather than rejecting realism, like Yeats, the later O'Casey, and early Eliot, he seemed content to allow reality to emerge from the concerns and speech of his subjects. Thus

Synge uses the drama not to exhort his audience like Shaw, or to lift them into an ideal sphere of contemplation like Yeats. Rather, it is a vehicle for activating that transient sphere beyond the self, with the dramatist serving only as an uninvolved spectator.

In his prefaces to *Playboy* and *Tinker's Wedding*, Synge places himself in the mainstream of realism. "It is possible for a writer to be rich and copious in his words," he writes in 1907, "and at the same time to give the reality, which is the root of all poetry, in a comprehensive and natural form." His use of nature, not only to establish a sense of place, but to form a solid basis for his characters' perceptions of permanence, permeates the plays. Yet Synge is not really a scientist by temperament, nor is his detachment from society much more than protective camouflage. His plays reflect both his sympathy with spontaneity and rebellious distaste for life's rigidities, achieving a "delicately balanced system of ironies, ambivalences, both of words and situation," [2] in T. R. Henn's words. For if Synge is a detached collector of backwoods folklore, he is also an engaged and analogizing intelligence, forever expressing his wonder at hearing "a story that is so full of European associations." As Ann Saddlemyer observes, to deny the inner needs of man's nature is to deny the reality out of which man springs.[3]

Synge's antipathy toward the thesis play stems from his interrelated attitudes toward creativity, the artist's function, and the conflict he reflected in his plays. Critics have failed to make much of his prefaces, so "deliberate, lapidary" they have seemed. No one has noticed how crammed with food and its appetitive delights they are. In the preface to *The Tinker's Wedding*, Synge gauges the seriousness of drama by the "pleasure and excitement" with which one takes in "the nourishment . . . on which our imaginations live." To go to the theatre for didacticism is like going to a chemist's or dramshop, where cloying liqueurs or drugs are dispensed. By contrast, the best drama (like that of

Jonson and Moliere) remains as timelessly fresh as "blackberries on the hedges." In his culinary metaphors, as in the famous eavesdropping allusion, when he took in "every speech . . . as fully flavored as a nut or apple," he yearns for reduction to a disembodied eye, making of that perceptive organ in turn a kind of seeking palate. It is as though looking at plays gratifies an unconscious wish to return to a preverbal life of looking at one's mother, taking her in through the eyes. As the psychologist Otto Fenichel has pointed out, to look at something may mean "to devour the object looked at, to grow like it (be formed to imitate it), or, conversely, to force it to grow like oneself." [4] So if Synge is a detached realist, allowing a flow of life and speech to proceed naturally, the way he positions himself and rearranges reality involves a comment on the efficacy of art. However objective he is, he is forever working to embrace the sensuous, vital, and spontaneous in his work and exclude whatever seems decadent, artificial, and mannered.

During Synge's lifetime he, Yeats, and Lady Gregory based their plays on folklore, all stressing the theme of transformation. But whereas Yeats's development as a playwright proceeds from the beginning through clearly delineated stages, Synge's diversity is remarkable, given the nature of his talents. His evolution from short to more lengthy, demanding plots was made tentatively at the expense of a great many discarded scenarios and laborious revisions. He had tried writing a play in German, set another in Paris, and left several verse plays unfinished. Along with his concern with refining an unchanging vision of objective reality, he deals with similar plots and immediately recognizable stock types: a youthful hero often affected with braggadocio and folly, a sexy but deceptively permissive heroine, heavy fathers, licentious or dolorous mother-types, and a complement of dunces, parasites, and drinkers. His situations are also traditional: a hero's oedipal struggle with a tyrannical father, the entertaining schemes and ultimate rejection of a tricky parasite, the resurrection of the old man (both as opponent and savior), a festive conclusion, and the victory of open over closed society. Within the typology of Northrop Frye's *Anatomy of Criticism*, *Shadow of the Glen* and the much more complex *Playboy* are the second phase or "quixotic" comedy, where a society is formed by or around a hero but cannot sustain itself. *Riders*, *Well of the Saints*, and *Tinker's Wedding* belong to a corresponding phase of irony, also quixotic like Menippean satire, conveying a powerful sense that experience is bigger than any set of beliefs about it. Finally, *Deirdre* is second-phase tragedy; it involves, like Shaw's *Saint Joan*, the destruction of baffled innocence in conflict with adult experience. Synge seemed to assume that if he approached his vision honestly, the appropriate form would evolve of itself.

Synge's stress on modes of perception suggests another reason for his antagonism toward Zola and Ibsen, who conceive of nature as neutral and divide their characters into good and evil. More influenced by the Greek and French classics than by his contemporaries, he envisions society as fallen and degenerate rather than malevolent, his characters' errors resulting not from villainy, but from their fear of sensate pleasure Thus they are drawn into conflict against their wills, driven by massive forces beyond their comprehension and control. This creates a crucial disparity between his men: the active and passive, his virile, confident poet-tramps and his frightened, insecure farmers or villagers. His more vigorous males commonly renounce hetrosexual love for homoerotic competition or aggression, as in work, games, and combat, followed by drinking or storytelling. They accept and idolize a woman's chastity because it demands the sublimation they embrace. In his early *Shadow of the Glen*, neither the tramp Nora accompanies nor the old husband she leaves comprehend her aspirations for freedom. She mostly provides an occasion for conflict they enjoy far more than any love or fidelity she could supply as she—like Sarah Casey in *Tinker's Wedding*—will soon discover. Synge's less aggressive males, on the other hand, succumb far more readily to childlike, sometimes alcoholic fantasies, the kind of drifting often associated with the mother's womb. Yet as Synge's imagery of food and its pleasures imply, man's hunger for love is so great that he can be baited, trapped, and engulfed. The matrix he must decide between sinking into or fighting his way loose from is usually envisaged as woman or her natural surrogates, capable of betraying him, petrifying him into marriage, swallowing up his restlessness.

As many critics have remarked, Synge uses all the devices at his disposal to adjust the claims of imagination to reason, fantasy to reality, the ordinary to the ideal. But these terms are too abstract. Rather, although both are often victims, it is man against woman or, within the personalities of both, aggressive and acquisitive vs. passive, accepting tendencies. His admirable characters like Bartley, the Tramp in *Shadow*, and Christy are trying to rise or grasp aggressively, perhaps achieving feats which will be recorded permanently in the memory of the folk. Or, like Nora Burke, Martin Doul, Maurya, Sarah Casey, and Deirdre, they are desperately trying to preserve a sensitivity and openness which the world would destroy. His weaker characters, on the other hand, are deluded by the belief that capitulation will end conflict, as Shawn in *Playboy* remarks: "It's the like of me only she's fit for, a quiet simple fellow wouldn't raise a hand upon her [Pegeen] if she scratched herself." In all his plays, therefore, Synge places one or two suffering, beleaguered Ironists within a circle of uncomprehending, insensitive Alazons or Impostors; a significant measure of his impact results from the pathos of fleeting recognitions, by most of his obtuse or brutal characters, that they in some sense are also victims, of the past, nature, or their own inborn follies. Conchubor, for example, is proud and blind in his assumption that he can stand between Deirdre and her predestined sorrows. But he too suffers from loneliness, frustration, and the bitterness of power without joy.

Riders to the Sea is a highly praised one-act, constructed with economy and cumulative inevitability. As in *Shadow*, Synge has presented a group portrait of isolated family life, although the author-persona has vanished. His musical training emerges in the way his characters detach themselves for solos, duets, and trios (against a group chorus of keening at the end) without anyone ever assuming the function of a protagonist. On the realistic level, the family faces a cruel dilemma: if Bartley, who is the last of Maurya's men, goes down to sea, the family may have enough to eat. But if he is persuaded to avoid its dangers, the family will go hungry. In strictly dramatic terms, Maurya, the matriarch of the family, struggles doggedly with Bartley, then with her daughters who conceal the death of Michael, and finally (successfully) with her bitterness toward the sea, once Bartley is returned drowned. Synge's characters treat even the imminence of death with commonplace gestures of everyday life, endowing their trivial activities with universality and personifying the impersonal and overwhelming forces of the sea. In the enormous attraction the sea exerts toward her lovers, it functions within the conventions of the White Goddess tradition. Like the archetypal temptress, it is inscrutable, cruel, and irresistibly fascinating to her lovers. They come to her seeking nourishment, rebirth, and love, but are fatally engulfed. Maurya's barrenness, symbolized by the emptied cup of holy water by Bartley's body, signifies a kind of mock victory. Having no more men to lose, she will suffer no more sorrow.

The Well of the Saints is Synge's first experiment with the three-act form and the closest he approaches a doctrinaire philosophical statement: the illusions of blindness are superior to the hypocrisies of the sighted world. Two blind beggars, Martin and Mary Doul, are granted sight by a wandering saint's application of holy water. Once convinced of their beauty by Timmy the

Smith and his fiancée Molly Byrne, they now find each other repulsive instead and are alienated by the shock. Martin is put off by work, disgusted with the ugliness of reality, and finally rejected by Molly Byrne whose beauty fascinates him. When the sight of both Douls fades again, they reject sight and flee the tormenting villagers for the south where, it is predicted, "the two of them will be drowned together in a short while, surely." On the conscious level, the play attacks the cruelty and rigidity of a peasant society absorbing a middle-class work ethic. Unconsciously, the play rejects the direct, visual, daylight experience of life for an indirect, aural, dark set of fantasies. One defends against a wish to see by distancing the rejections of adult sexuality into sound and scents, "hearing a soft wind turning round the little leaves of the spring and feeling the sun, and we not tormenting our souls with the sight of the gray days, and the holy men, and the dirty feet is trampling the world," Martin remarks. Blindness, the joys of nature, and escape (though into death) help the Douls feel that adult life is not violent, passionate, or sexual. But their illusions are mocked (perhaps) by the culminating celebration of Timmy's and Molly's marriage.

The Well is too static and predictable to be wholly successful, but Synge's central concerns emerge in it. His plots are deeply rooted in romance, though handled so ironically that moral norms are ambiguous. While in folklore a dragon guards a hoard, Synge's aged priests, fathers, and kings attempt vicariously to relive their lost youths through younger surrogates who must force or trick their elders into delivering up a "treasure" to them. These intangible yearnings for self-fulfillment are symbolized mundanely in Dan Burke's gold, food for Maurya's family, the holy water in *Well*, and rewards of brides and occupations in the later plays. In mythic terms, the questor is snatching a boon from hellmouth, as symbolized by entrapping cabins in *Shadow*, *Playboy*, and *Deirdre*, the dangerous river in *Well*, the voracious

sea in *Riders,* and the open grave at the end of *Deirdre.*
Usually, the questing protagonist receives a talisman,
like the priest's gift of invulnerability in *Riders,* the gift
of "beauty" conferred on the Douls, Sarah Casey's ring
and epithet "Beauty of Ballinacrae," Christy's magic
tongue, and the artifacts and safe conducts Conchubor
provides Deirdre and Naisi with. But in every case, the
elder's act of acquiescence, willing or not, is a sham.
He merely withdraws into the pretence of death or approval, waiting to trap or expel his antagonist. The
outer actions of the plays deal with the ordeals of his
questors, who experience a series of adventures, see
visions, and finally grasp transformation from mock
death, as in *Shadow, Tinker's Wedding* or *Playboy.* Or
they accept death in *Riders, Well,* and *Deirdre.* Invariably, however, social and personal goals are revealed to
be incompatible. As a result, society's most vigorous
and imaginative representatives are compelled to fash-
ion a purely individual identity.

The Playboy of the Western World (1907) is Synge's
masterpiece. In this play Christy Mahon is transformed
from a shy nonentity into a charismatic sex idol by the
reactions of some villagers to his oedipal story of mur-
dering his father. Beneath the appearance of the isolated
and impoverished village he chooses for his setting,
Synge has created a complex vision of the perennial
earthly city. His locale symbolizes the unregenerate
community forever exposed to the errant and self-destructive tendencies of the human will. Synge's world is
small, but perfectly proportioned, as T. S. Eliot
described Jonson's; his characters are flat, but they fit
their world perfectly. Ironically, the villagers' initial
horseplay foreshadows Christy's plight. Their attempts
to trap Shawn into spending the night with his fiancée,
the wild Pegeen Mike, is like Old Mahon's threat to
marry off Christy to his one-time nurse, "a walking
terror beyond the hills." Initially, Christy and Shawn
are doubles, oppressed by fathers and disdained by
their own social groups. Just as their contest for Pegeen

provides much of the surface excitement and suspense, the mood of the play is polarized by offstage eminences. The stern, moralistic traits of the often-cited priest, Father Reilly, constantly prompt Shawn's anxieties. For his part, Christy both rejects and attempts with growing success to emulate his father's masculine aggressiveness. Old Mahon is mythicized as passionate, rebellious, and untrammeled, "a man'd be raging all times, the while he was waking, like a gaudy officer you'd hear cursing and damning and swearing oaths."

Synge focuses on a single setting, making Christy's imagination rather than events in or outside the tiny shebeen the key to development. He also constructs each act on similar lines: Christy fixes in his mind a desirable self-concept, parodied by rapid changes of clothing and frequent uses of mirrors. His over confidence meets a comic reversal, recovery and recognition drawing together aspiration and felt reality. From the moment he is induced to confess his "murder," Christy is carried along rather passively by the villagers' unexpected delight and connivance, though aided by histrionic gifts for rhetorical embellishment and improvisation. The villagers' eagerness to hire a murderer as Pegeen's defender and leave the two alone springs partly from their view of him, in some sense, as a victim, as well as from their haste to attend a drunken wake. Yet, fearing tinkers, British police, and discharged militiamen who roam nearby, they vicariously savor Christy's criminal power and freedom, soaring collectively into fantasies of unpunished "murder or a bad, nasty thing, or false coining, or butchery or the like of them." Implacably hostile toward anyone too strong to need their approval, they seem harmlessly cowardly, prurient, and credulous. As long as they assist Christy's quest, we view them indulgently.

In their oblique courtship games, Pegeen manages Christy skillfully, alternately feeding his vanity with approval and rousing his anxieties by threats of desertion. Yet she is no more satisfied with her identity than

Christy is with his, and both begin to blossom in one another's idealized mirrors. Alone among his characters, following the practice of Jonson and Molière, Synge establishes a touchstone of common sense in the Widow Quinn. Having adopted the earthly and acquisitive values of her community simply to survive, she treasures the genuine vitality she glimpses beneath Christy's mask of heroism. And she alone warns Christy of the viciousness of mankind he too readily overlooks. Seeing the turning point of his life increasingly as the moment when he struck his father, he has simplistically condemned his former associates and idealized his present ones. Fortunately for his continued growth into manhood, the increasing strength of Christy's opposition lags a step behind his stage-by-stage growth in confidence. When his father unexpectedly appears near the climax in act 2, Christy having just resisted Shawn's desperate attempt to bribe him into departing, the Widow coolly intercepts Old Mahon and sends him off (temporarily) with a ruse. Her promises to Shawn to marry Christy and to Christy to help obtain Pegeen if suitably rewarded, extend the traditional roles of parasite and amused go-between. The multiplied bribes parody everyone's tendency to treat love as possession, reducing affection to a commercial transaction. Each game player drives toward entrapment of another while keeping his own options and freedom of choice open. In essence, Synge's play is about detachment and involvement, freedom and captivity, especially from and with images of ideal man and woman. Paradoxically though, what matters is contest rather than direct, sensuous enjoyment of the fruits of victory, as Christy exults early in the play: "It's fine luck and company I've won in the end of time—two fine women fighting for the likes of me."

Having gained a series of victories over his father, Shawn, and finally the offstage riders and carnival barkers, Christy again courts Pegeen in the flush of new vigor; disbelieving at first, she softens and yields to his poetic fervor:

If the mitred bishops seen you that time, they'd be the like of the holy prophets, I'm thinking, do be straining the bars of Paradise to lay eyes on the Lady Helen of Troy, and she abroad, pacing back and forward, with a nosegay in her golden shawl.

His heightened imagery of passion, like the increasingly mythic versions of his father-killing, recreates their personalities in more simplified, childlike, but idealized versions both of their love and the world as a whole. Although Synge subtly parodies the airy illusoriness of poetry, Christy's rhetoric is not only a source of pleasure in itself but a barrier against loss and impingement.

But when Michael James's blessing of their union is climaxed shatteringly by Old Mahon's unforeseen attack on Christy, Pegeen is totally disillusioned: "there's a great gap between gallous story and a dirty deed." Incapable like Martin Doul of accepting anything less than a transcendent uniqueness, she aids the villagers in Christy's capture—once he has struck his father again—and burns his leg to quell his struggles. But Christy has formed an allegiance to a mature identity he values more than life itself, symbolized by his refusal to accept a symbolically castrating disguise and escape in petticoats offered by the Widow Quinn. Finally seeing himself as a frozen mirror of his father's virtues, a comic symbol of immortality—"Are you coming to be killed a third time, or what ails you now?"—he leads his father away "like a gallant captain with his heathen slave." Though he lauds the villagers for assisting his transformation, Pegeen is left to bewail her loss. As with mother-daughter pairs who depart O'Casey's plays, Christy and his father, like Dan Burke and Michael Dara in *Shadow*, form an asexual, homoerotic couple. In Synge's case, they are men in flight from women into fantasies of endlessly diverting adventure. What may disturb audiences and critics alike is Synge's refusal to disguise, even in his endings, a deep anxiety that talk, homoerotic competition and affection, or stereotyped diversions may be inadequate defenses against engulfment by a threatening matrix, whether it be aggressive women, paranoid social groups, or a beautiful but indifferent nature. The personal choices made by the Mahons at the end, between love and freedom, mask the failure of a whole society to reconcile dominance and acceptance, life and the dream.

The language of *Playboy* could not be duplicated outside its setting, as Eliot predicted. But the work's stress on an identity formed through communal "play" affected Yeats's portrayal of Decima's search for an antithetical self in *The Player Queen* (1907–15). And O'Casey's *Cock-a-Doodle Dandy* owes much to Synge. The play also anticipates the tragicomic mixtures of surface farce and inner disvaluation, ideality and collapse, witty language and dissipating tension found not only in his Irish successors but in the best of modern European drama.

In *Deirdre of the Sorrows*, left unfinished at his death, Synge adapted a folkloric plot for the first time. Though his people move through a recognizable natural setting and speak Irish idioms, subdued since *Playboy*, society has disappeared into a symbol of precariously maintained social order, King Conchubor. And tension has broadened from attempts to merge identity into the ideal into a desperate struggle to defeat the unseen but inexorable forces of time and decay. As in ancient stories of Tristan and Isolde, Deirdre escapes the marriage Conchubor has planned by exile with Naisi and his brothers, The Sons of Usna. Yet her motives are suitably complex, springing from a wish to avoid being reduced to "a child or plaything," to seize a "sweet life" from childhood portents of sorrow, and perhaps, to evade the realities of maturity which she senses as a kind of death. Despite attempts to conceal the fact from one another, they find their life together not unpredictable and wonderful but boring and death-obsessed. Their return to certain betrayal and death at the hands of Conchubor springs from motives that drove Deirdre away in the first place, an escape from the unreliable, fallible body into an image of perfection:

The girl born the way I'm born is more likely to wish for a man who'd be her likeness . . . a man with his hair like the raven, maybe, and his skin like the snow and his lips like blood spilt on it.

Like Pegeen Mike in *Playboy*, Deirdre seems to crave an all-powerful, all-loving parent whom one could not judge in real terms at all. By going to their deaths, Deirdre and Naisi try to master erotic problems—like Nora and the tramp in *Shadow*, Martin and Mary Doul—by physical exertion. Their deaths also make an oblique appeal for love, a somewhat unfair coercion, by seeking out an undying, forever diverting affection. Deirdre proclaims:

It is not a small thing to be rid of grey hairs and the loosening of the teeth. (*With a sort of triumph*). *It* was the choice of lives we had in the clear woods, and in the grave, we're safe, surely. . . .

And she joins Naisi and his brothers in death as the possessions Conchubor has amassed to stave off insecurity lie in ruins.

Playboy and *Deirdre* use differing modes of construction. But both involve attempts to master ambivalence by splitting off erotic transport from competition, cloistering from wandering, engulfment from talk, art's preserving forces from time's disintegrating ones. By isolating pairs, one gains control over them. Synge's depth of contemplation, along with his energetic and complex defenses, permitted him to deal with fantasies his audience could not tolerate. He was bound to lose theatre and audience or sacrifice his art; O'Casey is the most spectacular example of an Irish successor who did both. While Synge never loses a keen hold on the Irishness of his subjects, he imbues his plots with a growing universality. Though even Yeats and Lady Gregory encountered an unbreachable reserve about the man, neither could write of him without admiration, leading to an inevitable sort of mythmaking about Yeats's efforts. Yet Synge's stature as a modern playwright fully justifies the image Yeats memorialized in his art.

5

Sean O'Casey

Although Sean O'Casey's later plays have never received fully satisfactory productions, his reputation as a dramatist rests on his earlier work, notably *Juno and the Paycock* (1925) and *The Plough and the Stars* (1926), staged at the Abbey. *Cock-a-Doodle Dandy* (1949), a romantic extravaganza written in O'Casey's seventieth year, is a possible exception. Because of his unabashed love of melodramatic devices, and particularly because of his self-taught reflections of the Bible, Shakespeare, and Dion Boucicault, O'Casey has been regarded with some justice as Synge's opposite. An urban primitivist in contrast with the sophisticated, well-read Bohemian, he is deeply committed to the power of impassioned, idiomatic speech to reform society. His seething resentments are spewed upon a puritanical Catholic clergy, the narrow-minded *petite bourgeoise,* and the De Valerian government supported by those twin pillars.

However, as O'Casey's rebellious quest for identity (reflected by two name changes) fixed on the craft and vocation of a writer, a double-layered personality came into view. Long before the Abbey produced *The Shadow of a Gunman* in 1923 when O'Casey was nearly middle-aged, his romanticism reflected a self which was essentially passionate, optimistic, and rebellious. Alluding to Bernard Shaw's *The Doctor's Dilemma,* a character proclaims his entrancement by the might of design, the mystery of color, and the belief in the redemption of all things by beauty everlasting. But this inborn expansiveness was countered by some of the cruelest, most painful frustrations a future artist has ever met in his formative years: the searing pain of eye infections which left his sight greatly impaired; a brutalizing slum environment of grinding poverty and degradation; and a Protestant heritage imposing upon him the anomalous role of "outsider's outsider." Perpetually dissatisfied with the shifting, weighty masses of native Irish conflicts, O'Casey successfully unified these diverse elements in his works only so long as his faith in their ultimate reconciliation in the real world lasted.

Nowhere is the tension between O'Casey's idealistic and analytic drives more evident than in his ambivalence toward the artist's role, craft, and powers, particularly as they are defined and expressed by words. His artist-personae treat poetry as priests do the Mass, using sacred language to bless, prophesy, or curse. Along with his countrymen, he regards the unseen spiritual authority of Catholicism with a mixed awe and dread. To a romantic individualist, moreover, nothing is so infuriating as the unreasoning subordination of "inferiors" to their social and moral superiors, an act of repression which, like the bending of man to God's will, was backed by the full authority of the Church. One bricklayer reminds another in O'Casey's late play, *The Bishop's Bonfire* (1955):

> Remember what your Canon said that when you served oul' Reiligan, you served God; so as I'm servin' Reiligan, by servin' me, you're servin' God, too.[1]

Both audience and artist respond to art viscerally, viewing books in particular as tools of the devil, undermining the moral rigidities of society. Reacting reflexively, "Captain" Boyle blames Mary's pregnancy on her reading in *Juno*, Father Domineer condemns Loreleen Marthraun's books as "Hell's bells tolling people away from the thruth!" in *Cock-a-Doodle Dandy*, and a bonfire planned to celebrate the bishop's arrival is stacked with "piles of bad books an' evil pictures on top of it . . . to go away in flames." No less emotionally, O'Casey's artist-figure seizes on books as potent antiauthoritarian weapons. In reading, the budding rationalist makes his mind his own rather than the Church's—still a live issue in Ireland, just as by writing books, he aspires to a kind of immortality outside the Church's sanction.

Unlike Shaw, whose novelistic stage directions and often intrusive personal opinions he reflects, O'Casey is not a systematic thinker. Yet he quickly perceived that in a capricious and willfully cruel world, submission to authority is invariably equated with connivance, escape from it with irresponsibility. Since it is not just a social system but life itself which arouses O'Casey's furious resentment, his lifelong, romantic commitment to communism masks an apocalyptic totalism. Too puritanical and repressed to fully explore man's naked cruelty, O'Casey divides his characters into two main types—deluded, humorless rebels and witty, innovative thinkers, those who embrace violence and those who attempt to withdraw from it. But whether victimizers or victims, almost all of his people are repelled by their own emotions and seek a haven of rest beyond the clash of endless turmoil.

Incapable of being either alone or alone with a lover, O'Casey's characters seek engulfment or isolation from sensation, conveyed at their extremes by fire and water symbolism. The flickering of one's inner aliveness may emerge as an impatient drive to magnify human destiny, to bring life to its conclusion. The intertwined deaths of Drishogue O'Morrigun and Edgar Hatherleigh in flaming, coffinlike airplane crashes in *Oak Leaves* echo the martyrdom of Ayamonn Breydon, whose bier is decorated with fiery roses. Only a fiery cataclysm, it would seem, enables the desperate idealist to grasp certainty from the one true Identity, which was Divine wrath. Yet in contrast to the poetic light by which the Dublin slums and its denizens are transmuted "to bronze an' purple by the sun" in *Red Roses*, the fire which entombs Jack Clitheroe in the burning Imperial Hotel symbolizes the destruction of evil cities.

Like fire, water symbolism projects radical antitheses of relief and impingement, depending on a character's relatedness to his group. Surrendering to drink, as O'Casey gave in to communist orthodoxy, was a means of controlling one's rebellious drives by submitting to a force larger than oneself. O'Casey's drinkers—"Captain" Boyle and Joxer, Fluther Good and Peter, the "Codger" and his cronies, among others—merge alcoholically with their worlds. Drink, one should note, is implicitly linked with floating in the amniotic fluid of the mother's womb. For his insecure authoritarians, particularly those who project their fears on societal scapegoats, normally pleasurable sensations threaten submergence in putrefaction. Father Domineer shouts in *Dandy*:

> How often have yous been told that pagan poison is floodin' th' world, an' that Ireland is dhrinkin' in generous doses through films, plays an' books!

In the early plays extremes of freedom and subjection are juxtaposed: Jack Boyle's regressive drunkenness stresses his family's vulnerability, while a sense of universal nullity qualifies the heroism of Clitheroe's sacrifice. But in later plays, extremes are treated allegorically, clarifying themes but impoverishing their ironies.

In his first-produced *Shadow of a Gunman*, O'Casey dramatizes a violent incident in the 1920 guerrilla warfare between the insurgent Irish Republican Army and the British Auxiliary "Black and Tans." His difficulties in sustaining a consistent tone throughout both acts, as well as unifying the exciting offstage actions with the ineffectual delusions of his titular antihero, are typical of apprentice work. However, the play is less important in itself than for what it foreshadows. Although it does not look very autobiographical, O'Casey is still present in disguise, split into the cautious and superstitious peddler, Seumas Shields, and the vain escapist Donal Davoren, whom the innocent Minnie Powell mistakes for a "gunman on the run." In writing the play, the author stands back from negative identity fragments, roles which tear him between empty poetic glamor and cowardly withdrawal. When Davoren allows Minnie to sacrifice her life for him, his vanity and self-centered mendacity are shatteringly exposed. But it is the character, and not the author, who is identified with a windy Shelleyan mysticism. By distancing himself from both deluded poetizing and heated nationalistic fervor, O'Casey has begun to subordinate ideas to their total dramatic context.

Like its predecessor, *Juno and the Paycock* is set during the continuing Irish upheavals, this time in 1922 while the Civil War raged on. As David Krause has shown, the radius of involvement has expanded to encompass a whole family.[2] Labored allusions to Shelley, Milton, and Shakespeare have dropped away. Although the beginning, middle, and end of the play are composed of the discovery of a "legacy," the family's reveling in it, and its loss, as Robert Hogan comments, O'Casey's debt to Ibsen is fairly deep.[3] In fact, the theme of *Juno* is so close to that of *The Wild Duck*— that only illusions can sustain life—that Krause has stressed the superiority of the realistic courage of O'Casey's women over the vainglorious cowardice of his men. This is an oversimplification. O'Casey has reflected not ethically on deluded actions or careful thought, but metaphysically on the very quality of existence. As a result, he has placed within the searchlight of his moral consciousness the irremediable schism between acquisitive drives and selfless acceptance, what one wishes were so and what is so. Figured behind the rather creaking melodramatic device of the legacy is the archetypal motif of Ireland as white goddess who—as in *Gunman*—ineluctably destroys her lovers. Seumas Shields had commented revealingly,

> Kathleen ni Houlihan is very different now to the woman who used to play the harp an' sing, "Weep

on, weep on, your hour is past," for she's a ragin'
divil now, an' if you only look crooked at her you're
sure of a punch in th' eye.

Thus to O'Casey's imagination, the condition of the
world of the play is symbolized by a body mutilated,
twisted and torn in every way, but in particular by loss
of covering. Johnny Boyle, Juno's activist son, loses the
use of his limbs, the trust of his former comrades, and
finally his life, a progression the author parodies with
the Captain's pains in his legs when a job appears, the
"theft" of his clothes by "Needles" Nugent, and finally,
the removal of the apartment's unpaid-for furnishings.

Throughout his early trilogy, O'Casey's characters
lead lives of virtual paranoia; neighbors repeatedly intrude to spy, mock, or steal; armed militants break in
to harass, arrest, and murder; and even the spiritual
world torments them with indistinguishable true and
false omens. The battered interiors of his crowded tene-
ments objectify the torn bodies of his victims while
symbolizing the country's terrible political and religious
divisions.

By placing an energetic and compassionate mother,
Juno Boyle, in the midst of a sick Irish society, O'Casey
creates the impression that the tragic inevitability of
the play was avoidable. Because the family is desperately
poor, Juno is primarily concerned with the numberless
ways of simply surviving. Although she possesses an
unread disdain for abstract theorizing, Juno is actually
testing everything—Johnny's militancy, her husband
Jack's refusal to contribute to the family's support, her
daughter Mary's love and work life—in the light of her
limited, traditional moral sensibility. Juno believes quite
simply that the good are rewarded and the evil punished,
or should be, in a morally organized universe. Ironically,
the two most impressive confirmations of her beliefs, the
first-act announcement of the legacy and the second-
act funeral of Mrs. Tancred's son, foreshadow the play's
disasters.

At her most enlightened, Juno recognizes that if the senseless violence affecting everyone in the tenement is "not our business, I don't know whose business it is." But without her knowledge and mostly before the play begins, Juno's values have been undermined by a tangled web of concealed or rationalized betrayals: Johnny has given away a fellow rebel, an act which his former comrades wish to punish; Mary has rejected Jerry Devine for Charles Bentham, who hopes the legacy he has drafted (in error, it turns out) will finance his training as a barrister; after Bentham rejects Mary for her poverty and ignorance, Devine does so for her pregnancy: the "Captain's" practiced malingering vitiates his paternal authority and support.

Juno's confrontations of the other characters, with her great but confused vitality, not only reveal her shrewd idealism but more deeply enmesh her in her world's shortcomings. To her family, each of them already compromised, Juno's probes arise as much from her voyeuristic drives, compensating her own frustrations, as from maternal concern. At the brink of economic disaster, the legacy appears, Juno's qualms are largely muted, and each character gains the isolating, self-destroying concealment he desires. By the beginning of the third act, from being the widest and most realistic consciousness in the play, Juno's role has diminished, leaving her unaware of the collapse of the legacy, Mary's pregnancy and desertion, or Johnny's mortal danger.

In the last act, Juno undergoes a Joycean epiphany as, one after another, the secure façades are stripped away from the bulwarks of Western society. Deserting her husband as worthless, she promises her daughter's unborn child "what's far betther" than a father—"it'll have two mothers," discarding the paternalistic family. The government's ineffectuality in preventing senseless violence is denounced in Mrs. Madigan's cries that "the Polis . . . is Null an' Void!" And the incorrigible viciousness underlying religious illusions is exposed in Juno's bitter plaint, "What can God do agen the stupidity o' men!"

Caught unwittingly in the collapse of society, Jack and Juno share responsibility for the debacle. For his part, Boyle had compulsively sought a warm, blissful state where no hard choices intrude, his moveable Saturnalia with Joxer implicitly commenting on society's niggardliness. Compassionate and witty as she is, Juno deeply resented the limitations of a passive maternal role. By hunting, spying on, and bullying her family, she effectively usurped her husband's role. Her replacement of Mary's absent husband involves the adoption of an oblique bisexuality her daughter will soon find irksome. Yet Jack has the last word in the play, returning drunkenly to the abandoned flat: "th' whole world's . . . in a terr . . . ible state o' chassis!" Petty and selfish as all humanity, he will yet survive. Boyle's antics paradoxically reveal him as both infantile and yet, accepting no trammels on his actions, also godlike. By avoiding any final judgment between striving and acceptance, heroism and compassion, O'Casey treats humanity in crisis with balance and objectivity.

In *The Plough and the Stars*, O'Casey widens the focus of conflict to encompass a whole city at war, while multiplying his antagonists to illuminate every aspect of his theme. As in *Juno*, the civil, religious, and ideological strife rending Ireland makes a seething battleground of the family, represented by Jack and Nora Clitheroe, their relatives, and neighbors. Weak and uncertain beneath his militant patriotism, Clitheroe is torn between the rebel cause and his quiet but increasingly dull family life. When his former rival Captain Brennan arrives with mobilization orders, revealing that Nora had burnt his commission, Clitheroe arms himself and leaves.

In the second act, as war fever grows, the slum dwellers reassemble in a pub where as before, the quarrelsome drinkers parody the inflated and inflammatory prose of the rebels. The Irish cause is personified by a silhouetted orator, an effective expressionistic device. In a demonic parody of the Mass, he exhorts his hearers to rebirth through an orgy of bloodshed and sacrifice, demanding

the homage of millions of lives given gladly for love
of country. And we must be ready to pour out the
same red wine in the same glorious sacrifice, for without shedding of blood there is no redemption!

It is almost as though the Irish rebels were seeking to
heal ancient Oedipal wounds by violence, freeing the
maternal body of Ireland from the rapacious, paternal
grasp of England. In a comic reversal of Clitheroe's
denial of love for duty, the ageing, gallant, but prag-
matic Fluther Good springs to the defence of a pretty
young prostitute. Once his tormentor, the Covey, has
been ignominiously expelled from the tavern by the bar-
tender, Fluther takes Rosie Redmond home to bed, and
the Citizen Army marches off to the attack.

The third act deals with the war itself, revealed in
excited reports of gory slaughter, tides of blood, and
crackling fire. But the mystic ferocity of the rebels has
unwittingly provoked a situation of tragic enmity destined to take on an impersonal, overwhelming force of
its own. When the British inevitably respond with
crushingly superior force, a simple binary pattern
emerges. An inexorable catastrophe is set in motion,
stripping rebels and bystanders alike of dignity, freedom,
and even their lives. The melodramatic revenge action
of *Juno*, where Johnny is killed for betraying a comrade,
envelops a whole people.

In an ironic parody of the outer plot, the quarrelsome
noncombatants mock and thwart one another up to the
very moment the rebellion falters. As in the plays of
Samuel Beckett, so much more distilled than O'Casey's,
the farcical misdeeds of his clowns heighten our sense of
a disvalued, incomprehensible universe. When the chaos
of the disintegrating Irish cause spreads into the slum-
dwellers' lives, they forge their conduct from adversity
like a group of "method" actors. Bessie Burgess had
once shrewishly ridiculed Irish loyalties, resorting to
eccentric aggressiveness to compensate her isolation.
Under fire, she quietly assumes a still critical, but

benevolent, authoritative role. Fluther Good also evolves, from a winning but cautious Falstaffian rogue into a courageous symbol of manliness.

Yet the war which fashions a bond of interdependence between the characters vitiates any effective exercise of their new-found heroism. Bessie quietly gives a cup of milk to Mollser Gogan, but the tubercular child dies; Fluther Good risks his life in a futile attempt to find a doctor, but Nora Clitheroe—who had frantically sought to drag Jack away from the barricades—loses husband, her stillborn baby, and finally her sanity; Bessie makes a frenzied attempt to protect Nora but is herself mistaken for a rebel sniper and shot to death. Since all the women are attached to a peaceful and congenial stability, they base their very beings on their men, themselves in flight from inner inadequacies.

In *Juno*, evil is done melodramatically by identifiable villains: thus a sharp disparity appears between human malevolence and the good but helpless spirit of the universe. In the *Plough*, as in Synge's *Riders to the Sea* and Shaw's *Heartbreak House*, malignancy is rooted in the heart of the cosmos. The whole galaxy appears suffused with malice, and fire drops from the very heavens. Injustice so pervades the play that conventional virtues are not only dubious but impossible. Complaining that antagonists are "not playing the goime!", both victors and victims of war emerge as incompetent, deluded mediocrities. In such a world, Fluther Good need only display a discreet pragmatism and a perceptive sensitivity to the foibles of others to be considered a "whole man" by the women of the play. Hedging bravery with natural caution, he intuitively adjusts his piercing skepticism to a flawed social milieu.

The play ends in Bessie Burgess's cramped, disorderly flat, stuffed with children's corpses, frightened fugitives, and then British irregulars. Like the legacy in *Juno*, the war resembles a malign practical joke which has gone beyond farce into living nightmare. To their comic horror, the captive men are herded away to custody in a

Protestant church. Not only are artificial class and religious barriers erased by war, but also the idealized
theocracy envisioned by the rebels. After Bessie's death
and Nora's departure in the care of Mrs. Cogan, two
uncomprehending British soldiers heat a kettle for tea.
A chorus of "Keep th' owme fires burning," ends the
play, as the flames of a dying civilization rise outside.
Their tea-time nonchalance may be, ironically, the
sanest of inadequate reactions to imminent universal
chaos. The play's implications seem more universal
than *Juno*'s, where the pathos of defeated women partly
obscures their responsibility for the catastrophe. In
Plough, O'Casey compresses within familial symbolism
a complex disparity between visions of heroism and the
ineffectuality of selfless actions, the gap between man's
antic delusions and his compulsive failures. Along with
his fully realized historical milieu, his preoccupation
with social turmoil, and his feeling for an ideal community of man, O'Casey places schismatic Ireland in a
wider setting that universalizes it.

Once O'Casey rejects his poet's hope for a productive
role in transforming society for the more modest goal
of theatrical recognition, the titanic contradictions he
had once imbedded in complex interrelationships melt
away. For all his apparent faith in creativity, the artist-
dreamers who appear in plays beginning with *Within
the Gates* (1933) exhibit curious disabilities. Ayamonn
Breydon in *Red Roses* is O'Casey's most explicit self-
portrait, an aspiring painter who transforms the Dublin
slums, but only momentarily. In a comic counterpoint,
Brennan o' th' Moor anticipates his magical feat by
secretly gilding a faded statuette of the Madonna, working a diminutive but longer-lasting "miracle." Breydon
feels compelled finally to renounce both art and the
love of his Catholic fiancée for a gratuitous martyrdom.
Society offers few roles to the artist and those few are
self-defeating, O'Casey seems to conclude: impotent
visionary, benevolent charlatan, or defeated rebel.

In the same plays, his artists' antagonists are as unrestrained as they are morally unprincipled, neatly countering good intentions with unbridled villainy. With no fear of effective retaliation, scoundrels like the fascist Kian in *The Star Turns Red*, Father Domineer in *Cock-a-Doodle Dandy*, and Manus Monroe in *The Bishop's Bonfire* unflinchingly commit murder. While O'Casey scorns the self-righteous pride and dogmatic narrowness of his ideologues, he secretly envies them their uncomplicated assurance, the approval of a reverential society, and their freedom from ordinary moral restraints—all of them attributes his artists desperately but futilely crave. Thus, O'Casey's social revolt, like O'Neill's and Brecht's, finds its target in the greed, the fatuousness and the sadism of society's agents; but his existential revolt is romantic, vitalist, and apocalyptic.

Cock-a-Doodle Dandy (1949) may be the most accomplished of O'Casey's later plays. It is also his most condensed, with its unity of setting and time scheme. In a blighted summer garden in back of the middle-aged Michael Marthraun's isolated country house, a trio of vital but frustrated young women try to establish a joyful and spontaneous regime, assisted by Robin Adair. Marthraun's young second wife Lorna, his grown-up daughter Loreleen from an earlier marriage, and the symbolically named Maid Marion form an inner group of *eirons*, purposely affecting ignorance in self-defense. Opposing them are a series of deluded impostors, agents of organized Irish obsessions: the greedy and ambitious Marthraun, Shanaar the fake prophet, the bigoted Father Domineer, and a frenzied mob of villagers. The clash between the two groups occurs when the women charm from the men's minds their repressed longings, filling most of the action with the pure slapstick of farce: horns sprout from the women's heads, a bottle of whiskey solidifies and then turns red-hot, chairs break beneath the men, a mysterious wind threatens to tear off the men's pants, etc.

The ubiquitous Cock of the title, symbolizing the spontaneous exuberance and fertility of nature, is less the source of the frantic activity of the play than an Ariel-like agent of Robin Adair. This messenger assumes a satirical but despairing Prospero-like role in the play, functioning as a hovering reflective intelligence or *raisonneur*—commenting or expostulating. On the comic level of the play, it is as though Robin were leading the convention-bound characters through a maze and showing them marvels meant to bring them true self-knowledge. But the attempt ends in failure, resulting in a neatly symmetrical ternary action: a fallen society is granted a brief glimpse of a festival world of license and renewal, usually available only through drink, dance, song, and the more lively arts. The dead hand of the past proves too strong, however. The vitalists are ostracized, and society returns unchanged to its former lifeless state.

The main or "serious" inner plot combines the joke of an older man's unmanageable young wife with the *Comus* theme of threatened chastity. Abetted by Lorna, her stepmother, Loreleen is "seeking happiness, an' failing to find it." Attempting to preserve her joy in life, Loreleen undergoes a series of ordeals. They rise in intensity from her father's misappropriation of her small legacy to reprimands from the village priest, Sailor Mahan's clumsy seduction attempt, and finally expulsion by a coarsened mob restlessly searching for a scapegoat upon whom they may vent their explosive lusts and greed. The crowd's perversity is heightened rather than abated by Father Domineer's cynical connivance. Despite the play's farcical hilarity, the society of the play is one of the most brutalized and irredeemable O'Casey has ever portrayed.

The Sailor Mahan, joined with Michael Marthraun in another of O'Casey's characteristic pairs of "butties," is pivotal in the action. As tight-fisted and incipiently lustful as his friend, he has attained more worldly success than his models, Joxer Daly and Fluther Good, introducing more ambivalence into his motives. His cautious skepticism toward sham makes him distrustful of both religious fraud and calls to sexual emancipation. At the same time, the natural sympathy with which he responds to the demands of his workers and the charms of a maiden is a softness which he, in his love of security and social acceptance, is only too inclined to suppress.

Freed from the restrictions of dramatic realism, O'Casey extends his vision of a forbidding universe: his cosmos is suffused by the spirit of a capricious deity who delights in the torment of its helpless human victims. The terror of such a being is personified in Father Domineer, while the fate of a whole society is suggested by the child Julia's mortal illness. Her hopeful departure for a cure at Lourdes at the end of the first act is balanced, crushingly, by her final hopeless return. As in *Juno*, *Plough*, and *Red Roses*, the play's two most vital women, Lorna and Loreleen, adopt mother-daughter roles, retreating from a hostile society to a visionary and unreal secret community. Their departure confirms Robin Adair's rather jarring response to Marthraun's despair: "Die. There is nothing else left useful for the likes of you to do." Inhibitions are the death of spontaneity, but disorder is the end of culture, O'Casey seems to conclude.

Except for his propagandistic set pieces, O'Casey's later plays, from *The Silver Tassie* to *Drums of Father Ned* (1958), increasingly deal with settled, isolated rural communities. The suffering, noble mother figure of the early plays is replaced by sexy, permissive young girls. Sensuality is pitted against the repressive agents of poverty, materialism, and guilt in losing battles. Yet the humiliations and torments of his "pure prostitutes," once subordinated to social malaise, are treated for their sensationalism, revealing an extremely naïve conception of sexuality. Along with his reversion to stereotyped romantic ideals of unlimited human freedom, O'Casey flattens his characterizations. Both passionate and confused, his earlier characters had tenaciously replaced their masks as quickly as reality had ripped them off, so powerfully had apocalyptic drives churned beneath the surface. In his later work, fixations once in conflict within personality are divided among an agglomerate of humour characters or *alazons*. His social groups, which degenerate quickly into mobs, are usually led by a rich, pompous local official in tacit league with a ruthless and hypocritical priest. Although his clowns and vitalists characteristically turn the pretensions of his impostors into a hilarious shambles, their devices— diverting, but usually unrelated to plot—are powerless to alter the enduring social anomalies. In O'Casey as in Swift and Juvenal, Eric Bentley suggests, "a furious desire to accuse, arraign, punish and reform" consorts "with a passionate conviction that accusation, arraignment, punishment and reform do not work." [4] His later plays are supposed to be imaginative, experimental dramas with no concessions to outworn tradition. But his casts increasingly fill with stage Irishmen, stock English villains, and excited crowd choruses worthy of Dion Boucicault.

In his masterpieces, *Juno and the Paycock* and *The Plough and the Stars*, O'Casey demonstrates a growing ingenuity and competence. He skillfully projects the tragicomic disparity between farcical aggressiveness and ineffectual yieldings within the cockpit of the family upon a nation recoiling against itself. But in his more disparate, experimental plays, beneath the joyous vitality which marks his characters' restless quests for innocence and freedom, grew a profound and restless frustration with life's rigidities, which he identified, in turn, with the limitations of the drama itself. Thus, his experiments with form, his excursions into expressionistic treatments of communistic uprisings or misty Irish folklore, represent attempts to deal with his own growing dissatisfaction with the vivid but wholly symbolic role of the artist. The more ludicrous the comic misdeeds become in his plays, the surer his humor contains an admission of failure, a resentful accommodation to things as they are. But it is for his earlier plays that O'Casey will be remembered, where he effectively dramatized the anguish of moral paralysis.

6

T. S. Eliot and Christopher Fry

The drama of T. S. Eliot is designed, like that of Yeats, to revitalize a minority, antinaturalistic tradition inherited from the Romantics. Wordsworth, Beddoes, Keats, Southey, and practically every English poet from Coleridge to Swinburne wrote verse plays. Most held the mistaken assumption that mastery of poetic language, plus a bag of theatrical tricks, would result in superb drama. Their failures were partial or total. Yeats and Eliot, with the possible addition of Christopher Fry, remain the only significant practitioners of this genre in modern English drama. Like Yeats, Eliot supports an idealistic, "non-Aristotelian" theatre: their protagonists are not battered to bits by social pressures, but have the insight and self-possession to make choices. The recognitions which their central figures achieve are dramatic *non sequiturs*, lifting them to levels of consciousness remote from their past experiences and the comprehension of their societies. But while Yeats frankly stressed the artifice of his theatrical conventions, he subordinated language, dance and music to a central situation. Eliot, on the other hand, initially saw lyric verse as the basis of drama, not just one of the tools which can be utilized by the playwright, "aiming at the same intensity at which poetry and the other forms of art aim." [1]

Eliot's powerful desire for unity, to merge with something permanent in the world rather than engage endlessly with flux, may account for statements such as:

It is ultimately the function of art, in imposing a credible order upon reality, and thereby eliciting some perception of an order *in* reality, to bring us to a condition of serenity, stillness, and reconciliation.[2]

It is reasonable to ask whether such an aim goes beyond aesthetic concerns toward an attempt to force ideological consistency onto his own unconscious dualism. While Yeats's esoteric and cumbersome system as amplified in *The Vision* is an extension of his subjective, evolving temperament, Christian belief helped Eliot find "objective correlatives" for his emotions and rationalize his aesthetics. In his attacks on power politics, an obsession with "but one law, to seize the power and keep it," [3] he seems more defeated rebel than objective observer. Although he supports a cultural order which is settled, provincial, and aristocratic in its lifestyle, his posture of opposition, his tendency to sharpen rather than soften contrasts, and his destructive and satirical wit hardly suit the passivity of a religious emotionalism. Therefore, Eliot not only reflects but shares the dividedness of his age. On the surface, his animus is directed against the looseness, materialism, and shallowness of a secular era; in the depths, against the formlessness of the universe (the "abyss" being one of his favorite metaphors) and the disorder within the human psyche. His social revolt is impeccably reactionary, focusing on a declared preference for the "classical in literature, royalist in politics, anglo-catholic in religion." [4] His existential revolt is individualistic, romantic, active, and rebellious. The conflict between the two modes of thought is common to the unacknowledged American aristocracy, such as the Adamses and the Eliots, and emerges in the dialectic of his art: a clash between the spiritual and materialistic.

Viewed abstractly, the act of the artistic creation is an "escape from" rather than into personality; it results from a complete readiness for the realization of the work, not from conscious fabrication of an artifact.

Yet just as Eliot is drawn in his criticism to the early seventeenth century in England, when cohesive forces were coming unhinged, his imagery captures the degeneration and numbness of human will. Although the tone of his poetry shifts from satiric to devotional after *The Hollow Men* (1925), metaphors of rot, deliquescence, and loss pervade his work; his characters fade and flake behind makeshift masks. Facing a fixed and ordered past as the future drags him into an incomprehensible milieu, Eliot instinctively retreats into self, his Sweeney remarking wearily,

> *I gotta use words when I talk to you*
> *But if you understand me or if you dont*
> *That's nothing to me and nothing to you.*

Accordingly, the protagonists of his early plays—Sweeney, Thomas à Becket, Harry Mounchensey—are byronic heroes, brooding, introspective, concealing secret guilts and obsessions.

Seeing man in the natural state as a Yahoo, not a noble and generous creature, Eliot agrees with Machiavelli, Arnold, and Newman that man's inborn stupidity and rebelliousness require the most stringent control. In *The Idea of a Christian Society* (1939), he visualizes the creation of an elite—who presumably overcome an inborn sinfulness through Christian humility—exercising a kind of spiritual guardianship over a tranquil and devout peasantry. He is a long-term optimist, but for the short term, only the most tenacious, dedicated efforts can preserve a saving remnant. As a result, Eliot turns his attention to the ordinary unaware but numerous theatregoers. Distracted by comic surfaces of incident and wit, such people might be beguiled toward spirituality through their senses:

> The audience, its attention held by the dramatic action, its emotions stirred by the situation between the characters, should be too intent upon the play to be wholly conscious of the medium.[5]

In the service of his beliefs, Eliot is as indebted as O'Casey or Synge to the art forms of the lower classes —melodrama, newspaper scandals, vaudeville farce, jazz rhythms, nursery rhymes, and ballads.

At the basis of Eliot's anxieties lies his horror of things running together, of clear boundaries between the self and the other objects being obliterated. R. P. Blackmur has commented upon the frequency in his work of physiological images to symbolize one's ways of knowing and the quality of things known.[6] Since in archetypal terms, the world takes on the aspect of a devouring trap or cage, like the open-mouthed monster of hell, Eliot repeatedly associates some dire penalty with sexuality; love leads directly to vulnerability, pain, isolation. Imagery of thirst, loneliness, and mocking voices, suffered while wandering in a wasteland, are the tangible projections of lovelessness, while anomie is ended by a wished-for withdrawal to a garden. Eliot's defensive strategies, like Shaw's, involve talking oneself loose from an enslaving matrix: Sweeney's anecdotes, Becket's sermon, Harry's confession. Or he can use logic to create barriers between categories: erecting hierarchies of levels of awareness, keeping the materials of art apart from one's emotions, separating philosophic wholeness from decadence. If all else fails, one flies upward toward God, the still yet turning wheel. Unlike Yeats, who tried to sink his mind below consciousness into the stream of the *anima mundi*, Eliot postulates a solid underpinning of myth beneath the appearance of change. As a result, his characters separate toward two main types: the vast majority who passively suffer disembodiment and the more conscious few who seek actively to wrench free from engulfment.

Still, Eliot's commitment to a unified community is too strong to permit him satisfaction with the private, antisocial aims of poetry. And his rationality is too hard, controlled, and urbane to allow him to embrace the looseness of an exclusively religious vocation. So if Eliot is a rebel, he is a rebel questing for community. Inevitably, the progression of his drama toward an acceptance of life's moral as well as emotional tolerability parallels a lessening of tension. His chorus, which experiences the crises of existence in their fullest subjectivity, makes up the only valuable parts of his pageant play, *The Rock* (1934), and provides the touchstone of reality in *Murder in the Cathedral*. But the chorus provides only an occasional response in *The Family Reunion*, appears once in *The Cocktail Party*, and then disappears.

Eliot was extremely interested in the living, colloquial rhythms of dramatic language, but approached form very abstractly. He was writing a drama of ideas based on a single concept, trying to appeal to an audience—after *Murder*—which was notoriously impatient of allegory. And while he was drawn to farce, with its creation of a distorted but self-consistent world, as found in Jonson or Dickens, he had great difficulty converting intellect into passion. His passages of dialogue seem fragmentary, and interaction between characters often appears puppetlike as though manipulated by unseen levers. Although his society tragicomedies beginning with *The Family Reunion* (1939) aim at the serenity and stillness of Shakespeare's later romances, the evil and corruption which their moods of reconciliation enclose are oddly illusory. His characters seem repeatedly freed from guilt rather than from the consequences of real sin, as in *Cymbeline* or *Tempest*.

Eliot's early *Sweeney Agonistes* is entitled "Fragments of an Aristophanic Melodrama." Written in the form of a satirical comedy, it presents a farcically exaggerated situation alternating play and song. Two frivolous lower-class prostitutes, Dusty and Doris, pass the time in a flat provided by a Mr. Pereira, a mysterious and threatening offstage presence. After finding ominous portents in a deck of cards, a parody of religious faith, they welcome four businessmen as guests. In the second "Fragment," Sweeney's threat to carry Doris off to a "crocodile isle" works out his vision of a withdrawal to innocence. Lyric interludes by the oblivious visitors are followed by Sweeney's parody of rebirth, a macabre story of a murderer who kept the body of a girl in a Lysol bath. Although his oblique attempt to convey insight lapses, Sweeney foreshadows the plights of Becket and Harry Mounchensey, who form centers of consciousness within circles of uncomprehending mediocrities.

The incomplete *Sweeney* resembles Yeats's practice of tying and then untying a knot, stripping away all extraneous elements. But in *Murder in the Cathedral*, Eliot utilizes a hypothetical ritual structure which has no living tradition either in society or the theatre. His immobile, deeply contemplative Becket maintains the steadfast course taken by Sophocles' protagonist in *Oedipus at Colonus*. And the sequence of temptation, illumination, and martyrdom suggests the abstractness of *Everyman*. *Murder* also takes up the Elizabethan focus on a pivotal historical character, metaphysical verse suspending the extremes of incantation and meaning, and even a Shavian touch of farce (from *Saint Joan*) in the murderers' prose defenses. But Eliot has deliberately unified the play's action, tone, and motifs around a demonstration of the invisible truth behind martyrdom.

In the first half of the play, the Chorus of the Women of Canterbury, three Priests, four Tempters, and Thomas voice their differing anxieties aroused by Becket's danger. The Chorus suffers mindlessly, intuiting the approach of the murderers in terms of violation; the metaphorical texture of their speeches creates an underpattern drawing together the Waste Land, the seasons, beasts and birds, everyday tasks, and the blood of redemption. After the Priests voice their reasonable but circumscribed fears for the temporal church, a series of Tempters objectify Thomas's inner conflicts. He is tempted by the lures of sensuous pleasure—by "kissing time below the stairs," by compromise with the King for secular power, and by acceptance by an aristocratic elite. In summing up Thomas's relinquished past, the Tempters amplify the partial masks he had assumed, only to discard them for something both more vital and more permanent, power to "wind/ The thread of eternal life and death."

When a fourth Tempter unexpectedly appears, echoing Thomas's paradoxical words to the Chorus—"You know and do not know, what it is to act or suffer"— Thomas is staggered. In his attempts to find reality not in the mirror of the world but in the mirror of his mind, he reflects his creator's dividedness. Wishing to fuse himself with an unimpeachable outside power, he yet fears being swallowed up by roles, an anxiety projected upon metaphors of voracious, devouring animals. Thus the conflicting interests in the play comprise not only the orders of nature, mind, and charity and three parts of society, but make up a vision of an irretrievably torn self and environment, schism within and without.

After a chorus of response by the Tempters, Priests and Women, Becket resolves the acting-suffering paradox with a renewed commitment to martyrdom. Although no rationale is provided for his illumination, his new assurance turns a potentially destructive pride into an instrument for grace. The pattern will recur in the other plays, as in the transformation of the Furies into figures of benevolence in *The Family Reunion* and in the evolution of the "guardians" from busybodies into helpmeets in *The Cocktail Party*. Thomas's rejection of contemporary cynicism about martyrdom, termed the "senseless self-slaughter of a lunatic," frees him from the entrapping historical process of predictable consequences envisioned by the fourth Tempter. At this point the play's action is virtually completed.

Becket's Christmas Day sermon, which is a more general demonstration of the paradox of martyrdom and rebirth, is directed to the theatre audience. Although his personality remains dim, the sermon suspends the action between 1170 and 1935, universalizing it. It also provides a metaphoric axis for Thomas, the still point of the world that moves around him.

The second part of the play amplifies the consequences of Thomas's choice through the helpless agonies of the Priests, the drunken act of murder by the Knights, and the Chorus's final acceptance of the spiritual significance of Thomas's sacrifice. The speeches of the Knights, demonstrating another kind of mistaken reason, confirm the irreconcilability of worldly and eternal values. Even though Eliot's use of choral groupings, varied rhetorical and rhythmic patterns, and allegorical abstractions "distances" the play from third-wall realism, Thomas's basis of reality is convincing. We deduce Thomas's change of heart and final decision from our experience with his dramatized actions, rather than through revealed truth, replacing Eliot's theological paradoxes with our own, more skeptical psychological ones. From this point of view, Becket closely resembles Coriolanus, the hero of a play Eliot considers Shakespeare's most successful one. He is an individual of great integrity. But his temperamental unwillingness to accept the compromises imposed by society imprison him in that jealous selfhood. He is capable of single-minded action only when abstract issues pitting secularism against the will of God can be transformed into mutually exclusive Manichean essences. Failing when he must mingle himself with others, he succeeds only when he is on his (or God's) own. It is the other side of the paradox, of course, that Eliot intends to stress.

The Family Reunion (1939) was written to appeal to a wider, necessarily secular audience. Eliot assembles an archetypal family in a contemporary setting, the symbolically named Wishwood, to await the return of Henry Mounchensey. His mother Amy has held off death only by her determination to hand on the estate to him. When Harry appears, pursued by Furies suggested by the play's source in Aeschylus's *Oresteia*, he reveals the murder of his wife to everyone's disbelief. Warned off by the apparitions from seeking escape in sexual love with Mary, once intended for him, Harry turns for understanding to his Aunt Agatha. She reveals how his father had once plotted to murder Amy and the unborn Harry, combining the theme of original sin with a curse on the House of Mounchensey; but Agatha had dissuaded him. Harry now sees that he must accept his "inner" self which he had sought in memories of a childhood in the "rose garden," that he cannot escape his culpability in his father's guilty intentions. With that, his Furies turn into the "bright angels," and Harry leaves in a rejection of the estate which means Amy's death.

Eliot later found Amy a far more compassionate figure than Harry, whose escape out into society hardly seems more selfless than his earlier disastrous marriage or his return to Wishwood. Despite the play's flaws, all the motifs in Eliot's drama emerge in *The Family Reunion*. His protagonist, who is tormented by clouded parentage and a hidden crime, is coming out of or going into exile. Becket's alleged malfeasance in office, Harry's murder of his wife, the Chamberlaynes' sexual peccadilloes, the spate of abandoned children in *The Confidential Clerk*, and Lord Claverton's hit-and-run "murder" and desertion of a mistress in *The Elder Statesman* are all sins by intention. Except for *The Confidential Clerk*, their guilts materialize in versions of interfering "furies." To clarify the direction of his life, hoping to subsume the selfish and spiritual levels of being, Eliot's protagonist withdraws to refuges or rejoin family groups, or both. Sometimes he fuses his identity with a lost or substitute father, as Becket, or Harry Mounchensey, Colby, and Michael Claverton do. Or he may withdraw, Becket to France, Harry to childhood memories, characters in *Cocktail Party* and Lord Claverton to sanatoriums. Although his crimes are imaginary, his guilts are not. So with his acceptance of culpability for his share of others' mistakes, he isolates himself from family and society. Despite his growing acceptance of the possibilities of warmth in marriage, the ways of the world and sainthood remain incompatible. Neither joy nor glory have much place in Eliot's world, leaving "death and suffering," Lionel Trilling has concluded, as his "only means of conceiving the actuality of life." [7]

Eliot's greatest commercial success, *The Cocktail*

Party (1949), illustrates the risks he ran in the theatre. He dropped the mythic apparitions, the static choric responses and obtrusive verse of *The Family Reunion*. His grasp on theatrical mechanics has improved, and his source (in Euripides' *Alcestis*) effectively buried. Like Shaw, he imbedded an "inner" spiritual change within an "outer" action of intrigue, suspense and sexual pursuit. As a result, any interest in his ideas is at odds with his theatrical appeal. Initially, Edward Chamberlayne is trapped into hosting a cocktail party by the unexplained desertion of his wife, Lavinia. Stung by the mocking congratulations of an unidentified guest, later revealed as the psychiatrist Sir Henry Harcourt-Reilly, Edward recognizes his dependence on Lavinia's aggressive, domineering character. In her absence he feels petrified, "reduced to a thing." Too preoccupied with mere survival to risk genuine intimacy, he had sought self-esteem from the idolization of a mistress, Celia Coplestone. For her part, she had loved Edward's mask, an idealized image of a powerful, vigorous man. Discovering his dependence on Lavinia, she ends their affair.

In a brief Strindbergian clash, the Chamberlaynes penetrate on another's façades, perceiving that both of them have deteriorated within the cocoon of marriage. Apart from Edward, Lavinia has become disoriented and depersonalized: "Yesterday I started some machine, that goes on working and I cannot stop it." Edward's dependence on Lavinia has, in turn, drawn him away from the real world and engulfed him in a dream life: "Hell is oneself, Hell is alone, the other figures in it merely projections." Like Harry Mounchensey, he experiences doubts about his autonomy, blurring distinctions between inner and outer anxieties: "There is nothing to escape from and nothing to escape to. One is always alone." The Chamberlaynes thus form two halves of a single personality, each incapable of functioning without the other. Finding them "exceptionally well-suited to each other," Reilly persuades them to "make the best of a bad job."

Celia is too burdened with a sense of sin to turn outward toward marriage. Warned by Reilly that both marriage and sainthood bring one into contact with reality at the cost of loneliness, she chooses the other alternative provided by the therapist. As her counselor foresees, she embarks on a religious quest which leads her into a nursing order and then to martyrdom by crucifixion. As in *Murder*, the characters are distributed among three mutually exclusive groups: Celia in the order of charity; the "guardians" Julia, Harcourt-Reilly, and Alex in the order of mind; and the Chamberlaynes and Lavinia's lover Peter Quilpe in the order of nature. Although *The Cocktail Party* is the closest Eliot had yet come to an alternate mode of life to martyrdom, no contemplation of intimate human relationships is allowed for his most vibrant, highly introspective people.

As the play progresses, its Christian imagery arises unobtrusively from the situation, gradually pointing toward its spiritual meaning. Its primary metaphors involve sight and blindness, light and dark, supporting the three metaphorical conditions of blindness, half-sight, and full vision. As Denis Donoghue has pointed out, these conditions are exhibited, respectively, by Edward, Julia, and Celia.[8] Yet ambiguities in the concept of spiritual guardianship appear to undercut the spiritual superiority exercised by Reilly, Julia, and Alex. The psychologist D. W. Harding has concluded that Reilly has erred not only spiritually, in denying ordinary people the same choice he offers the potential saint, but professionally, in failing to offer more than advice to the seriously neurotic Chamberlaynes, whose situation is not the "human lot."[9] From the outside, the guardians' drive to "see into" the disorderly yet presumably spontaneous desires of others compensates for their own starved and unsatisfied states of existence. Eliot's difficulty in seeing that intellectual curiosity is a desire like any other, regardless of the rationale, is part of the susceptibility to illusion he shares with the rest of mankind, despite the systematic effort he has devoted to amplifying his Christian optimism.

In his last two plays, *The Confidential Clerk* (1953) and *The Elder Statesman* (1958), Eliot's assumptions undergo little change. In his next-to-last play he relies on the complications of farce, distributing several lost children among their rightful parents with the aid of a convenient *dea ex machina*. Although the central parent figures, Sir Claude Mulhammer and his wife, Lady Elizabeth, form a more sympathetic union, their would-be son Colby chooses a career as a second-rate organist rather than becoming Sir Claude's heir. Like that of Harry Mounchensey, his choice of identity is based on the person of his true father. *The Elder Statesman* traces the efforts of a retired politician, Lord Claverton, to come to terms with the hypocrisy he has adopted to conceal an inner emptiness. Pursued by two ambivalent associates from the past who remind him of hidden mistakes, he finally confesses his shortcomings to an adoring daughter, freeing her to marry. He loses his son to a questionable career abroad, but Claverton agrees to pay the price. He goes off to die in a garden outside the sanatorium to which he had withdrawn. Even though Eliot seems to have mellowed in his growing acceptance of human love, he never manages to extend his grasp of artistic unity from the brief, closely textured lyric to a unified, dramatic conception of character. Like Brecht and Wilder, he has consistently devised his plots and selected his characters to unfold an idea, to direct our attention to an invisible and undiscussible reality beyond earthly appearances. In his developing career in the theatre, he has tightened his mastery of continuity, flow, and plotting by sacrificing conflict, character evolution, and the sensuous presence of discernible poetry.

Christopher Fry's career as a poetic dramatist overlaps that of Eliot's. But where Eliot's construction is focused and ritualistic, Fry's appears panoramic and historical. The frankly religious basis of their work results in a marked allegorical deployment. But Fry's more humanistic and exuberant outlook shifts his stress from his older contemporary's concept of disparate levels of spiritual consciousness in a Manichean universe to a less forbidding outlook. For Fry, as for Wilder and Shaw, evil is a consequence of man's consciousness that he must die and that the supreme good is life. A significant part of his efforts was devoted to a series of religious festival plays dramatizing Biblical motifs. In *A Sleep of Prisoners* (1951),[10] he linked Old and New Testament episodes in a series of expressionistic dream events, and his next-to-last play, *Curtmantle* (1961), treated the three-way struggle between Henry II, Eleanor of Aquitaine, and Becket. His comedies, on the other hand, are designed as tragicomic romances, all of them set in a timeless or distant past. Drawing upon the conventions of the comedies of manners established by Congreve, Sheridan, and Wilde, his best play, *The Lady's Not for Burning* (1948), also has its gay and serious couples, its panoply of farcical stock types, dance-like changes of mismatched partners, and the last-minute escapes from death and violation. In the end, two shrewd young women catch two clever but reluctant young men who have been their destined spouses throughout the play. Like Eliot's comedies, it catches the mood and temper of Shakespeare's later romances, yet his characters are Shavian. And like Pirandello and Anouilh, Fry has invented a fairy-tale world to win our consent to his ideas, mixing in enough reality to compel our belief, with sufficient fantasy to persuade us of his characters' sincerity.

In *Lady*, Thomas Mendip has returned from soldiering abroad. Oppressed by guilt and self-loathing, he loves life too much not to resent its shortcomings. When he encounters a young, beautiful woman suspected of witchcraft, he immediately confesses, hoping to end his life by saving hers. Like Shaw's St. Joan, Jennet Jourdemain is eccentric but charming, with a firm grip on life. In a farcical trial, the town's befuddled Mayor disappoints both of them, denying hanging to Thomas while sentencing Jennet to be burned. By playing off Jennet's romantic visions against Thomas's grotesque apocalyptic metaphors, Fry exposes the ludicrous short-comings of both legal process and martyrdom within a disturbed, chaotic society.

Like Eliot and Chekhov, Fry permits his action to unfold in a rather leisurely way through a succession of social ceremonies—homecoming, departures, troth-plighting, and sanctifications. And it is typical of both his and Eliot's practice to link the mundane Christian allusions to a deepening awareness of their spiritual import, resulting in a rich and complex allusiveness.

By staging an eavesdropping scene, Fry retains an unwavering focus on an intense debate between Thomas and Jennet. Their discussion is compelling not only through the inherent interest of their ideas, but through the incompatible efforts of each to keep his freedom of action and to influence the other. Attacking Jennet's grip on life as a deception, Thomas plays devil to her saint, finding beauty in the universe no evidence of a deity behind it. Yet once Jennet impresses Thomas as a sensitive, poised visionary rather than simply a frightened, deluded victim, their roles are reversed, and he plays Adam to her Eve.

At this point the action is virtually over, although Fry ingeniously conceals the fact with a festive party, a series of comic chases and exaggerated seduction at-temps, and a twist in the plot which saves Jennet from burning and unites the lovers. Jennet's supposed victim enters to parody both the slain god of the ancient vege-tation rites and the *deus* of Euripides. His "resurrection" completes the death of the others' illusions. While Thomas has received from Jennet the will to live, she has accepted conversion to the mysterious riddle of ex-istence. The conclusion confirms one of Fry's crucial concerns in his plays: the women who stand at the dramatic center of his comic plots represent a "higher," though not as in Eliot, a different kind of love than his men achieve. And while an excessive concern with bodily senses leads his "lower" characters into lust, avarice, and destruction, their vices are usually transposed into aspiration, self-sacrifice, and sublimation by the influence of his "higher" characters. Even though the evil from which his characters are delivered is usually quite absurd, it is by no means invariably harmless. Nor do his characters, at their best, defeat evil; they endure it for the sake of love.

In his drama, once his early experiments with choral interludes in *The Boy With a Cart* (1939) have dropped away, Fry skillfully modulates the tone of his verse to reflect character. Yet he shares Eliot's problems in sustaining tension within many of his more lengthy speeches. As in his subsequent tragicomedies *Venus Observed* (1950) and *The Dark Is Light Enough* (1954), *Lady* presents complexities, degraded heroes, and contrived solutions. The conversions which his characters undergo occasionally seem inconsistent with the human lusts, greed, and irrationality that move with so little check toward burnings, hangings, rapes, and warfare. Yet even though Fry has sometimes seemed wordy, overly optimistic and lacking in conventional kinds of conflict, he has more than compensated with vital and compassionate characters, the vision which assimilated contemporary issues to timeless themes, and some of the most sprightly language to enter the contemporary British theatre.

The impact of poetic drama on the contemporary English theatre has been confined to the efforts of Yeats and Eliot, with an afterglow in Fry. In their philosophic and religious attitudes, they fought a rear-guard action against a naturalism whose lack of heroism, poetic elegance, and beauty they bitterly resented. In view of the failures of such luminaries as Browning, James, and others to adjust their talents to the exigencies of modern theatre, Eliot's degree of success was remarkable. His imaginative grasp of the weight of history, his ear for the nuances of disparate voices, and his memorable phrasing were recognized early in his literary career. Never expansive or dilatory, more skilled at juxtaposing "blocks" of poetry than unifying an entire play around character, the virtuosity he managed to develop bespeaks an enormous effort of will. Refusing to repeat either his successes or his failures, Eliot learned by examining each of his earlier plays how to improve the next one. A modern audience pursuing escape or titillation was bound to find the stringencies of orthodox anglo-catholicism eccentric or repellant. So Eliot concealed his message behind an appealing surface of incident, hoping to lure his auditors toward an understanding of the motives behind martyrdom and Christian grace. Without foregoing his stature as a self-critical craftsman, he managed a degree of acceptance many lesser show merchants have found enviable. Unlike Shaw, he never sets out to prove anything: he assumes the truth of his beliefs and gears his fictionalizing to the purposes of an oblique, though convincing demonstration. And because he wishes to illustrate a common denominator, the variety of analogous experience he tries to assimilate is both larger than his allegory can usually sustain and too constricted to permit him, as his career progressed, to endow his protagonists with a convincing array of choices or motives. Most damaging to his stature as a dramatist is his unwillingness to examine his own religious illusions as piercingly as he anatomized other creeds, whether materialist, humanist, fascist, or Marxist. But he submitted his theories of drama to the astringent test of creation and production. And because his aspirations were high—if not so single-minded as he pretended—he deserves to be judged by his own standards.

7

The Moderns
Osborne, Arden, Pinter, Wesker, and Whiting

By common consent British drama renewed its claim on literary eminence on May 8, 1956, with the premier of John Osborne's *Look Back in Anger*, his first play to reach the London stage. The success of his play opened the floodgates for the emergence of a remarkable and diverse group of young dramatists including such original talents as Harold Pinter, Arnold Wesker, John Arden, and many others. Nothing remotely approaching the loose cohesion of an earlier group of Anglo-Irish playwrights could be discerned, with their interest in folklore and myth, the wrenching conflicts of Irish nationalism, and poetic enhancement of spoken idioms. What the more recent dramatists opposed, however, remained in many respects the same: a middle-class theatre of escape. Terence Rattigan functioned as H. A. Jones and A. W. Pinero had in the 1880s and 90s, French imports and Shakespearean revivals played to the boulevard, and the average theatregoer flocked to revues, musical comedy, and updated melodrama. Nearly all the new experimenters, however, were left-wing, rebellious, and contemptuous of the prevailing "conventional wisdom." Almost none were university trained, some had worked in or around the theatre, and many kept up a running association with working-class and peace movements, experimental theatre groups, the movies, and television. The provincial and socially oriented art theatres such as those of Joan Littlewood and Arnold Wesker suffered a fate similar to those of a long line of similar enterprises, providing a spurt of vitality but succumbing to under-financing and lack of a strong continuity of management, though George Devine's Royal Court Theatre is an exception. This flexible and imaginative establishment was responsible for Osborne as well as works by Arden, Ann Jellicoe, and the early works of N. F. Simpson, and it managed to spread an aura of respect throughout the profession even though, as John Russell Taylor remarks in his highly influential book, *Anger and After*, the lead in the new drama passed elsewhere almost at once (after 1956) "first to Stratford, E., then to the provinces (though in the case of Wesker, with the Royal Court's active encouragement), then to television." [1] So crowded with promise is the last decade and a half that only a few of the more prominent young dramatists could be treated in any detail, notably Osborne, Arden, Pinter, Wesker, and Whiting.

Osborne's *Look Back in Anger* [2] created an enormous stir, especially after its impact and box office were magnified by the televising of an excerpt midway through its run. Yet the play now seems more notable for a remarkable harmony of its content and mood with prevailing anxieties and antipathies among a rising generation of young British than for any formal breakthrough. Osborne has echoed his critics in finding it "a formal, rather old-fashioned play," with its naturalistic box set, well-timed entrances and exists, and sensational curtains. The oedipal overtones of his triangular character groupings recall parallel situations in Williams' *Streetcar Named Desire* and Shaw's *Candida*, to which he alludes, and Osborne has since acknowledged the influence of Williams, Jean Anouilh, and D. H. Lawrence. However, the traditional patness of the well-made form is upstaged by a burning, energetic, and (to much of its original audience) exhilarating tirade carried on virtually non-stop by Jimmy Porter, the central figure. He shares a cramped, dingy attic flat with his wife Alison, and most of their living arrangements with Cliff Lewis, who helps him operate a sweet shop. Within the bored lassitude of a Sunday afternoon in the Midlands, Porter lashes out restlessly at the "posh" newspaper reviews, middle-class dullness, the monarchy, Britain's imperialist pretensions, and a myriad of other targets. The brunt of his anger is borne, however, by his wife Alison. Her only defense through four years of abuse has become a pose of imperturbability, which Jimmy incessantly chips away at by attacks on the supposed vicious self-assurance of her aristocratic heritage, the hostility of her parents toward him, and the breaches she makes in his insecure selfhood. His dominance of the stage marks a strong tendency in Osborne to reduce minor characters to "feeds" for a vocal and deeply frustrated but potentially creative protagonist.

After a scuffling match between Jimmy and Cliff ends by burning Alison on her iron, Jimmy leaves. Alison then confesses to Cliff she is pregnant, news Jimmy would resent:

> He never stops telling himself that I know how vulnerable he is . . . In the morning he'd feel hoaxed, as if I were trying to kill him in the worst way of all . . . Jimmy's got his own private morality, as you know. What my mother calls "loose." It is pretty free, of course, but it's very harsh too.

But her attempted confession to Jimmy is thwarted by a telephoned announcement that an old friend, Helena Charles, will join them, plunging Jimmy into a rage directed (unknowingly) at Alison's unborn child:

> If you could have a child, and it would die. . . . Please—if only I could watch you face that. I wonder if you might even become a recognisable human being yourself. But I doubt it.

Unlike Alison, Helena accepts middle-class standards both more firmly and more superficially. As her old friend sinks deeper into exhaustion and despair—"All I want is a little peace!"—Helena rises to each of Jimmy's challenges, delighting him, while probing the motives underlying the frank exchange of affection between Alison and Cliff. Acting from mixed motives of indignation, hostility, and envy, Helena secretly sends for Alison's father to take his daughter away. The defiant departure of both women for church elicits a long, painful reminiscence by Jimmy of his father's death from wounds in the Spanish Civil War, climaxed by the shattering news that an old woman he had frankly admired for her unabashed ignorance lay near death from a stroke. But Alison refuses to accompany him to the hospital, a final gesture of desertion.

The following evening in his absence, Alison's father arrives for her. In view of the play's unremitting attacks on Establishment illusions, Colonel Redfern is a curiously sympathetic character, gentle and perceptive if saddened by the passing of his world. With their departure, Jimmy and Helena find themselves alone. After sharply attacking one another, they fall into bed together in what one critic has called an "instant relationship," typical of Osborne's reluctance to depict the organic growth of passionate attachments.

The last act audaciously repeats the setting and stance of the first one, except for Helena's replacement of Alison at the ironing board. Only sensuality holds her to Jimmy, resulting in a much more relaxed mood. As a result, Cliff feels cut adrift and leaves, to be followed by Helena once Alison returns, having lost her baby. Claiming no rights, Alison pleads, "I don't want to be neutral, I don't want to be a saint, I want to be a lost cause. I want to be corrupt and futile!" Alone once again, Alison and Jimmy take up the childlike game of bears and squirrels they have played intermittently throughout their marriage, suggesting that both their suffering has led to a temporary catharsis, serving only as exercises in futility. Although critics have sometimes seen a new beginning for their marriage in the ending, such a view seems too optimistic. Rather, after a brief respite, their interflagellation seems likely to resume with new vigor and venom.

The very range and diversity of Porter's targets sets up a radical disequilibrium between the sharpness of his rage and the diffuseness of his targets, between the damage inflicted on his ego and the defenselessness of his most palpable victims. "To be as vehement as he is is to be almost non-committal," Osborne notes. Despite his lament that "there are no good causes left," Porter has failed to fit into such loosely organized groups as vacuum cleaner outlets or jazz bands. Only confessionals, tirades, impromptu histrionics, and sex provide temporary solace; he is never seen at his sweet stall. His set pieces take their appeal less from their justness than from their metaphorical brilliance, emerging mostly in imagery of craving or appetite or their diversion into disgust and repulsion. At the root of both his oral splendors and social impotence lies a mingled fascination and abhorrence of woman, seemingly felt forever: "I learnt at an early age what it was to be angry—angry and helpless." As dangerous objects of lust, they seem best approached when dehumanized or helpless, something controlled and mastered by men. Porter's consequent longing for purification, for rising up from a tainted milieu, seems almost pathological. It is the vividness of his drive rather than the tangibility of either source of or respite from rage that Porter manages to communicate.

Osborne's next play, _The Entertainer_ (1957), portrays the final defeat of an aging and callous night-club entertainer within an experimental framework. Scenes from Archie Rice's rather sordid act alternate with those set within his family like vaudeville numbers, detailing Archie's advanced state of moral and emotional estrangement from his family, his profession, and his once idealistic hopes. Although Lawrence Olivier's presence in the lead role buoyed the play's theatrical success, Rice's collapse is never clearly linked with the downward slide of Britannia which it presumably parallels. _Luther_ (1961) followed disastrous excursions by Osborne into musical comedy and television. Along with Erik Erikson's psychoanalytic study, Osborne used Luther's actual words, constructing a series of rapid, panoramic scenes spanning an entire career. Yet the great reformer's charisma and vision, to say nothing of his dividedness toward an entrenched aristocracy and his own authoritarian instincts, are crowded out by a literal stress on his various ailments and neuroses.

Inadmissible Evidence (1964) may be Osborne's firmest achievement to date. His protagonist Bill Maitland is a failing attorney who finds himself, with a panic-stricken clarity of insight, on the verge of disintegration. An initial dream sequence establishes Maitland's attitude of self-incrimination, alluding to the quick-witted though mediocre man he once was and looking ahead to his escalating loss of grip in the next two days, each occupying an act. To the Judge who serves as a personified superego, he confesses having corrupted witnesses and alienated affections. Yet as the title implies, the link between Maitland's wrongdoing and suffering remains indistinct. The other characters in the play are, for once, perfectly situated in their flatness to elicit the blend of isolation and self-absorption Bill exhibits. And the framework of the legal office routine merges with the interior monologues by which he conducts the probing dissection of his anxieties, while providing a self-evident level of reality with which he tries ineffectually to cope.

Maitland's fitful wrestling with the humdrum activity of his floundering legal business manifests the terror of his growing isolation: taxis and caretakers ignore him, his subordinates are disaffected, and he seems able neither to avoid his clients nor to deal with them. His heavy drinking, repetitive sexual affairs, and overuse of drugs all seem attempts to dull a galloping insecurity. Ironically, he seems most alive in his intermittent, often malicious attacks on society, though like Porter's, his immediate targets are defenseless or uncomprehending, a hapless clerk or secretary. In the second act Maitland's growing apprehension emerges from a series of one-sided interviews, with each of his female clients being played by the same actress. Each confrontation works variations on the theme of frustrated sexuality which provides a complex symbol of combined punishment and reward. Maitland's rambling and introspective idiom coincides perfectly with his introjection of the roles of his clients' husbands, overlapping with telephone conversations (possibly also imaginary) in which he repeatedly, desperately tries to "plug in" to reality. An interview with a homosexual client, John Maples, accents disabilities they both share: a resentment of women without any compensating attraction toward men, an overwhelming sense of drift, a virtual welcome of entrapment. Maples, prostrate with self-recrimination, yearns for confessions, for finality. But the interview, like the play itself, ends inconclusively. Maitland brushes off his mistress's solicitations and lapses into impassivity, both fearing and welcoming an end: "Well the Law Society or someone will, sometime. . . . I think I'll just stay here. . . . Goodbye."

More like Macbeth than Hamlet, Maitland has lost all potential for greatness, finding himself faced with dismal alternatives: enduring increasingly devastating shocks or passively slipping into oblivion. His continued tirades against society, like Jimmy's fulminations, Archie Rice's lewdness, or Luther's heresies, are symptoms of an inner compulsion to commit outrages bringing on either punishment or affection, breaking through isolation in either case. Like Macbeth, Maitland identifies with mother figures so powerfully that his female clients, family members, and mistress coalesce, blurring lines between his inner self and reality. The pervasive atmosphere of dream dominating the second act resembles the surrealistic fantasies in *Macbeth*, drawing Maitland away from life and engulfing him in irreality. Only by mistreating women, cheating in law, and bitterly attacking society's stupidities can he (like Porter) achieve an independent identity. Like Macbeth, he seeks to resolve a confusing dualism between his society's imperatives and his own desires, between his actions and society's judgments, but the attempt fails, leaving him with Macbeth's mental suffering but none of his sense of retribution.

Since *Inadmissible Evidence*, Osborne has written historical melodrama (*A Patriot for Me*), updated Lope de Vega (unsuccessfully) in *A Bond Honored*, turned out a pot-boiler in *Time Present*; in *Hotel in Amsterdam*, he manages an impressive degree of ensemble portrayal without resolving old problems of overplotting. Yet midway into his career, Osborne's language remains among the most striking and idiomatic in the English theatre, conveying however the frustration and bitterness toward lovelessness felt by his protagonists far more effectively than it sustains any genuine dialectic. He has had difficulty in doing without outworn formal devices such as fortuitous pregnancies, pathetic death scenes, and stagy reversals. Yet if none of his plays has individually achieved the stature of Pinter's *The Homecoming* or Arden's *Serjeant Musgrave's Dance*, Osborne's histrionic gifts are great, and he has learned from experience, if somewhat erratically. As a playwright whose characters project the agony of isolation with drive and compelling fantasy, he is rivaled only by Pinter.

John Arden's career overlaps those of Osborne and Arnold Wesker in some respects. His public pronouncements have been radical, favoring causes such as pacifism and antiimperialism, and his plays utilize topical elements like the British health and housing schemes, anticolonialist incidents in Cyprus, and behind-the-scenes diplomatic maneuverings in Katanga. He has been as prolific and experimental as Osborne, writing children's plays, agitprop, television and radio drama, histories (*Left-Handed Liberty*),[3] an adaptation of Goethe's *Goetz von Berlichingen* retitled *Ironhand*, melodrama, and pantomime. While the conventionality of Osborne's plots is a critical cliché, hardly anyone among Arden's predecessors except Shaw and Eliot has so closely studied the dramatic tradition. Despite the diligent nurturing of the English Stage Company, he has attained little commercial success and seems to be stuck with the reputation of being a "difficult" dramatist. The reasons may lie more in the stereotyped expectations of his audiences than in his stagecraft. His characters descend directly from comedy and melodrama, although he undercuts their reality at the same time that he depicts it. While his plots are as intricate and confused as those of Jonson, reflecting the moral chaos of his fictional societies, they are easy to follow. Even when his language reflects illiteracies as in *Live Like Pigs* (1958) or sixteenth-century Scots dialect in *Armstrong's Last Goodnight* (1964), his idiom is firmly sinewed and authentic. The surface of his plays is suffused with the joys of gaming, irruptions of lyricism, and dancelike exuberance. Yet the reality below appears stubbornly resistant to change, even corrupt. Paradoxically, the dramatist he most resembles, Brecht, has had little direct influence, Martin Esslin believes. They are rather "kindred poetical talents following common models in a more distant tradition—Elizabethan drama, folk song, popular theatre of all kinds."[4] Although Arden seldom approaches the depth of Brecht's revulsion toward human instincts, he also views society as an excrescence upon nature, foundering upon the conflict of irreconcilable desires.

What most sharply separates Arden from Brecht is the "barrier to empathy" Brecht consciously seeks to erect between audience and work, the better to encourage his auditors to judge the conflicts in the play critically and reach a verdict. If Arden creates a similar effect with "alienation" devices such as songs, pantomime, and masks, his plays are among the least doctrinaire in the British theatre today. Not only are author-personae missing from his plays; he is extremely reluctant to envisage a world polarized by good and evil in opposition. Instead, "the private self" clashes ceaselessly with the "organizing, abstract, equally self-interested" action of politics, Richard Gilman has pointed out, not only externally but deep within character. The conflict of individuals with social groups, wayward spontaneity with order, is complemented, Gilman continues, by the confrontation of a deadly impulse toward purity with "the impure, flawed, capricious and uncodifiable nature of reality beneath our schemes for organizing it." [5] Arden's uncertainty about moral imperatives, the doubt and skepticism which endows his clowns with stature and his heroes with criminality, blocks the empathy of his audiences.

Despite his legendary difficulty, Arden's tragicomic plots pivot on a simple device: the "biter bit." This simply binary form uncovers the impersonal forces engulfing his characters, although Arden is as fond of misplaced letters, broken vows, and other plotting devices as the most inveterate "well-made" playwright. Complementing his ironic reversals is a pattern he identifies in a note to *Live Like Pigs*. In this play, a group of wild, undisciplined nomads, the Sawneys, clashes with a more settled family, the Jacksons; both their standards of conduct are valid in the right context, but incompatible. The Sawneys' existence, in turn, is complicated by the incursion of an even more eccentric group, affecting the Sawneys as the Sawneys do the Jacksons. From a distance, Arden's plotting suggests the surface confusion and formal perfection of a furious country dance: individuals, couples, and trios join one group and then another, revolving within and then without rings of dancers. By subordinating plot to characterization and incident, Arden diverts our attention from logic to motivation, making his audiences suspend their judgments of the action.

Rather than viewing individuals subjectively, personifying states of mind as the absurdists do, Arden presents human beings collectively, J. D. Hainsworth points out.[6] To conclude that ideals perish and the amoral prosper is to oversimplify Arden's sophisticated plotting, however. A close bond exists between Arden's rootless antiheroes, Krank (of *The Waters of Babylon*), the dilapidated Crape in *The Happy Haven*, Sir David Lindsay, the King's herald in *Armstrong's Last Goodnight*, and the buffoonish Blomax in *The Workhouse Donkey*. Despite differences, such characters apply their considerable gifts to self-presentation. Yearning for self-sufficiency, they mask deep feelings of insufficiency beneath claims for discipline, often perpetrating malign practical jokes. Krank's rigged lottery, Musgrave's plan to "undo" five fatalities by "doing" twenty-five civilians to death, Crape's connivance in the inoculation of a doctor with his own elixir, and the different types of blackmail applied by Lindsay and Blomax fit the pattern. Frequent changes of clothing, exemplifying their psychological disguises, manifest their determination to strip others of masks while retaining their own intact. With few exceptions, their plans fail or achieve only a temporary success. There are no conversions in the plays, implying a haunting Sisyphian sense that nothing is ever satisfyingly completed. Lindsay remarks on the entrapment of a troublesome rebel: "The man is deid, there will be nae war with England: this year. There will be but small turbulence upon the Border: this year." Consequently, man is stripped of dignity, friends, clothing, life, and even (as in *Musgrave*) the flesh on his bones, if not of hope and determination.

Serjeant Musgrave's Dance (1959) is Arden's best-known, most controversial play. The title character is a stern, uncompromising moralist whose aim emerges late in the play: since five colonials died following the shooting of a soldier, twenty-five of the boy's townspeople must die. He and his tiny band of deserters pose as recruiters, but their aim is complicated by disunity and a coal mine strike. Attercliffe opposes all wars, Hurst is a sadistic malcontent, and Sparky considers only his comrade's pointless death. Viewing them as strike-breakers, the miners try to steal their weapons, and the local power Establishment cynically hope to recruit troublemakers into the army. Out behind and around them, an unseen Nature suffers the fallen state of society, its canals frozen, roads blocked, and telegraph lines broken by the grip of winter.

In a pub where the soldiers bivouac, Mrs. Hitchcock

and her eccentric helper Annie hope to stir the town
back to "life and love," provoking Musgrave into
warning:

> Our work [is] drawn out straight and black for us, a
> clear plan. But if you come to us with what you call
> your life or love—*I'd* call it your indulgence—and you
> scribble all over that plan, you make it crooked, dirty,
> idle, untidy, bad—there's anarchy.

Disciplined and puritanical, Musgrave fears women
will choke off his desperate flight toward God into a
purer, less earthbound matrix: "Brothers in God—and
brothers in truth." Beneath his surface self-possession,
he is a confused improviser, seething with frustration
and aggression. He has never revealed his plans even to
his followers, since to do so would acknowledge their
freedom to follow him.

The turning point of the play is Sparky's death in a
quarrel over Annie in the stables. Not only are his sur-
vivors unnerved by Musgrave's disregard, but the incident impresses the serjeant anew with the randomness of
experience so resistant to human control. What he
yearns for, ultimately, is not a cruel bloodbath, but—
through the organizing energies of the mind—a symbolic affirmation of divine order:

> My prayer is: keep my mind clear so I can weigh
> Judgement against the Mercy and Judgement against
> the Blood, and make this dance as terrible as you
> have put it into my brain. The word alone is terrible:
> the Deed must be worse. But I know it is Your Logic,
> and You will provide.

Galvanized into action by news that troops have
been summoned, Musgrave launches his "recruiting
rally" in the town square. After loading their weapons,
Musgrave hoists his dead comrade's skeleton aloft,
breaks into a grotesque dance, and announces his
homeopathic cure: to purge his country's imperialist
madness by turning "it on them that sent it out of this

country." Paradoxically, what most angers him about England's colonialist ventures is not the contempt for supposed inferiors or brutality it unleashes, but the breakdown of logic into random, incomprehensible violence: "You see, the Queen's Book, which eighteen years I've lived, it's turned inside out for *me*. There used to be my duty, now there's a disease—." But his props fall away: Attercliffe deserts and stands against the muzzle of the Gatling gun, Hurst is shot by the arriving dragoons, and Musgrave is betrayed by the Bargee who had brought them to the town. "We're back where we were," a miner remarks bitterly. Musgrave had hoped by embarking on his messianic mission to "uncouple" his self from his actions, logic from the unreliable emotions, but the maneuver fails. Mrs. Hitchcock supplies a moral to the play, paraphrasing Musgrave's earlier warning:

> Look at this road: here we are, and we'd got life and love. Then you came in and you did your scribbling where nobody asked you. Aye, it's arsey-versey to what you said, but it's still an anarchy, isn't it? And it's all your work.

In a cosmos racked by social cataclysm, a search like Musgrave's for the source of malaise is bound to seem myopic and self-defeating.

In the years following *Dance*, Arden has produced a cornucopia of plays, including *Armstrong's Last Goodnight* (1964), possibly his masterpiece. The fallen politician Butterthwaite who had appeared in *The Waters of Babylon* is seen, still in power, in two television plays, *Soldier, Soldier* and *Wet Fish*; *The Workhouse Donkey* portrays his disgrace. Like *The Happy Haven*, a highly-formalized mixture of prose and verse, *Workhouse Donkey* brings social groups into conflict within a tightly knit social microcosm, concluding with the reduction of single-minded idealists to powerlessness. For *Left-Handed Liberty* (1965), Arden turned to a dramatization of climactic incidents in the reign of King John, written under commission to commemorate Magna Carta. He has also written children's and community dramas followed, in 1969, by *The Hero Rises Up*, based on episodes from the career of Lord Nelson.

Armstrong's Last Goodnight dramatizes the attempts of James V of Scotland to impose fealty on a set of unruly, boisterous border freebooters in the sixteenth-century. The world of the ballads has been invoked in the play, providing (in Susan Shrapnel's words) "a body of hard, strong, simple images and actions, suitable for understanding on the stage, but also capable of depth and variety of meaning." [7] Sir David Lindsay as the King's emissary pits his practised subtlety against John Armstrong of Gilnockie, whose energetic unpredictability has thwarted the most ingenious schemes to tame him. No heroes or villains are revealed by the maneuverings between rival clans, borderers and Crown, Scotland and England. Instead, as Lindsay remarks, the action reveals first one and then another of the "varieties of dishonor."

Given as much to emotional loyalties and direct, intuitive responses as to vulgar self-display and guilt, Armstrong threatens the less spectacular and more calculating order sought by an adolescent, as yet untested King. He must be crushed not because his ambition but his vitality is excessive, shaking a nascent, insecure realm struggling to be born from the carnage of Flodden Field. Lindsay's task is complicated by Armstrong's entrapment and murder of a royal vassal just before the laird is offered a royal lieutenancy, cancelling out the royal proclamations of outlawry. Armstrong's disabling stutter—except when sexual passion frees his tongue—differentiates him thematically from Lindsay who both reduces and magnifies himself as "the King's tongue and the King's ear," clearly phallic symbols. Lindsay repeatedly compares his task to the cutting of the Gordian knot by Alexander and, in another allusion, pairs himself and Armstrong within the struggle-of-brothers theme, instructing his secretary McGlass, "Jacob, Sandy, never Esau—let Gilnockie be your Esau." Lindsay is as audacious and courageous as Armstrong, but more self-controlled and devious, never revealing more than his function requires. Assuming that effective governance requires a continuous illusion, he manipulates the costumes he wears as shrewdly as he modulates his diplomatic and psychological disguises. His repulsion toward the body's "hairy sweat and nudity," appealing only to a torturer, the Creator, or an infatuated mistress impells him toward political manipulation as an art: present everywhere in its effects but visible nowhere except in the person and panoply of royalty.

After Lindsay has offered Armstrong the rewards of loyalty, persuading him to repudiate and thus weaken his dissident lord, the situation is inverted, creating a series of ironic reverberations. The turning point of the play is brought on as Lindsay's mistress and Armstrong rouse one another's passions in a courtship game. To Armstrong's richly associative imagination, his mingled gesture of arrogance and surrender is linked to his entrapment and death of a rival, Lindsay's initial proffers of reward, and even his own dimly glimpsed fate:

> I'm in my sark and my breeks w'nae soldiers, nae horses. As there were nae soldiers wi' David Lindsay, when he stood before my Yett. Am accoutrit convenient for ane passage of love. Or for execution.

As Lindsay had appeared to him, so the Lady embodies "ane knowledge, potent, secret" of sensuality, providing analogous paradigms of diplomacy, love-making and brute violence. Were Armstrong's services not demanded, he concludes, but requested "in humility as ane collaborate act of good friendship and fraternal warmth," they would be freely rendered. In a dramatic reversal, Armstrong's brother-in-law discovers his infidelity and pledges silence in return for collaboration in another border raid, signaling the collapse of Lindsay's policy. The drastic slippage of his political influence is arrested by a personal calamity when an unhistorical

Lutheran evangelist stabs his servant, a fairly transparent contrivance. The dying McGlass indicates a solution to Lindsay's problem, pointing up the emissary's underestimation of his adversary:

> Ye did tak pride in your recognition of the fallibility of man. Recognize your ain, then, Lindsay: ye have ane certain weakness, ye can never accept the gravity of ane other man's violence. For you yourself have never been grave in the hale of our life!

Deceptively repeating his original blandishments, Lindsay tricks Armstrong. Dressed outlandishly in finery to acknowledge the King's friendship, the borderer is instead condemned to death by hanging; the tree on which he dies withers and fades as "an examplar" of faithlessness. The closeness of his own escape confirms Lindsay's intuition that royalty symbolizes but can never finally incarnate invisible ideals of social discipline. Although Armstrong's innocence and virtue are undercut by his wily deceptiveness and brutality, a kind of moral justice is seen to outlast the corruptions of power politics.

Like Yeats and Brecht, Arden uses song, dance, mime, and gaming to restore outpourings of vitality to an overrepressed society. The powerful drives toward self-presentation in his plays, balanced by an equally strong skeptical caution, reflect his vision of a society suffused with crosscurrents of idealism, sensuality, and discipline, all at odds. Only by identifying with his passionate but confused rebels can he keep his optimism alive; by sympathizing with their destroyers, he keeps his grip on that necessary order by which society, morality, and art alike channel the chaotic flux of imagination. His characters live and move within a close milieu of overlapping desires and consequences, providing individuals and groups alike with great depth and balance. His willingness to employ moral allegories and parables, to celebrate the lasting traditions of society as well as the excesses of individuals, makes heavy demands on his audiences' sympathetic openness. At mid-career, Arden matches impressive promise with an already significant contribution to British drama.

Along with John Arden, Harold Pinter is one of the most innovative figures in modern British theatre. The wide-ranging, self-indulgent anger of Osborne's heroes and the evenly balanced clashes of order and individualism in Arden have no place in the spareness of Pinter's isolated rooms, last refuges of menaced nonentities. His characters are rootless and isolated, fearful that some usurper will enter the warm and womblike sanctuaries they have made their own. Intrusion is often enough to traumatize Pinter's victims whose crimes, like those of Kafka's characters, are never revealed. As in Beckett, another of Pinter's acknowledged sources, the settings are dilapidated and impoverished; his plots begin virtually at the moment of crisis. Typically, a disturbed refugee or two, a vague but growing sense of disquiet, and a vast and inchoate vacuum surrounding a room provide Pinter's basic situation:

> Two people in a room—I am dealing a great deal of the time with this image of two people in a room. The curtain goes up on stage, and I see it as a very potent question: what is going to happen to these two people in the room? Is someone going to open the door and come in? [8]

Active as a dramatist since 1957, Pinter began writing plays after a decade of acting. He has produced to date a number of revue sketches, five film scripts, two radio plays, five television plays, two one-act plays, and three full-length dramas. He and Edward Albee, on opposite sides of the Atlantic, remain the foremost dramatists of the absurd in English. His plots stress energetic but pointless movement; his characters are flat, stereotyped, and dreamlike, often resembling those of archetypal gangster movies of the 1920s and 30s; and his language mirrors the random, repetitive, and cliché-ridden talk of the ordinary unaware individual. In comparison with John Osborne's Bill Maitland or the most battered,

terrorized victims of Arden's drama, Pinter's characters
are unusually vulnerable and dessicated. Neither society, nature nor some form of belief provides any solace
for lives they discover to be, in rare moments of perception, "senseless, absurd, useless," [9] Martin Esslin
has characterized the world view of existentialism. "If
Pinter's plays seem to lack the rich tonality of Chekhov's
words," John Lahr has remarked, "it is because, in his
view, Nature gives us back no image of ourselves and
words, no matter how sensuous, are finally imprecise." [10]
In an era which seems to demand social commitments
from art and artists, Pinter is an apolitical artisan
interested only in his craft. He has refused to accept the
postulate of well-made playwriting that man can be
wholly known or the consequences of his actions fore-
seen with any certainty. In the traditional mode of the
Romantic artist, Pinter has stressed the mystery and
incomprehensibility of reality lying beneath the extremely accurate, realistically textured surfaces of his
plays.

Pinter's first full-length play, *The Birthday Party*
(1957), written after the one-acts *The Room* and *The
Dumb Waiter*, is typical of his early practice. The action
is set in a run-down, out-of-the-way seaside boarding-
house supposedly operated by Petey Boles and his wife
Meg, who is slovenly and rattle-brained. As is usual in
Pinter, the plight of a whole society is represented by
the metaphor of a house. Always realistically functional
but symbolic, by the end of the play it has become a
trap or cage. The Boles's only guest is Stanley Webber,
who claims to have been a concert pianist. Meg's at-
tentions to him are so smotheringly effusive as to verge
on the incestuous. After the neighborhood doxy Lulu
frightens him with a seduction attempt, he suffers an
ever greater shock. The two gangsters from *The Dumb
Waiter* arrive, incarnated as a nervous, sinister Irishman
McCann and a gregarious, showily unctuous Jew, Goldberg. They immediately agree to help Meg celebrate
Stanley's birthday (although he insists it is not) and un-

nerve him with a stichomythic inquisition, a foretaste of their use of language as power. At the party Stanley is blindfolded in a game of "blind man's buff." As the lights flash off and on, the increasingly disoriented Stanley tries to strangle Meg and then rape Lulu, attacks on sexuality he identifies obliquely with his predicament. Like the blindness which afflicts Rose in *The Room* after Bert kills the blind Negro Riley or the pain Edward feels in his eyes in *A Slight Ache* (1958), the breaking of Stanley's glasses by the gangsters symbolizes an assault on his virility. The next morning McCann and Goldberg take Stanley away, clean-shaven and helplessly catatonic, a mysterious punishment he accepts. Though he had fought back at first, Stanley had never tried to escape, viewing appeal to the oblivious Meg as futile.

In Pinter's plays, a victim always faces impingement or actual ejection from a temporary circle of familiarity and warmth. His culpability may be obscure, but he accepts his guilt and consequent punishment, establishing one of Pinter's basic patterns, "in place of another." The gunman Gus becomes his partner's victim in *The Dumb Waiter*, Flora forces a turnabout between her husband Edward and the dummylike matchseller in *A Slight Ache*, a couple alternate roles as spouses and betrayers in *The Lover* (1964), and Ruth takes the place of the dead Jessie in *The Homecoming* (1965) and replaces her husband Teddy with his father and brothers, even all men, it appears. In play after play, ambiguously paired men are introduced, linked as brothers, partners, or antagonists who "compete cooperatively" in a variety of ways. The archetypal fear that sight of one's double forebodes death never seems very far from the situation, although the violent deaths of Riley and possibly Gus are internalized or mocked in Pinter's later, more sophisticated efforts. Often, one member of a couple is far more quick-witted and articulate than his partner, who lags far behind verbally, providing a farcical pattern of disjointed, nonsensical interchanges and *non sequiturs*.

When women appear in his plays, variations are worked on a central oedipal situation. Rose in *The Room*, Meg in *The Birthday Party*, Flora in *A Slight Ache* and his later heroines parody the White Goddess archetype by appearing by turns unattainable, undesirable, or available to all. As Pinter's development proceeds, his women's sexuality becomes more and more prominent. If they are absent, as in *The Dumb Waiter* or *The Caretaker*, his men share maternal roles.

Behind his often mystifying dialogue, so close in form and impact to vaudevillian line-bouncing, is the problem of verification. His characters may contradict themselves or others regarding their "past" lives, flare into combat on slight provocation, or respond passively to the most grievous taunts; questions of fact remain unresolved or irrelevant; motivation may be inadequate or absent altogether. "Each of his plays," Kelly Morris has remarked, "produces a bizarre clash of conceptual expectations with Pinter's asocial intentions (in any morally corrective sense) and his non-realistic techniques." [11] While Ruby Cohn, for example, has concluded that Pinter's drama "savagely indicts a System which sports maudlin physical comforts, vulgar brand names, and vicious vestiges of a religious tradition," [12] Pinter has warned against an excessive desire for verification:

A character on the stage who can present no convincing argument or information as to his past experience, his present behaviour, or his aspirations, nor give a comprehensive analysis of his motives, is as legitimate and as worthy of attention as one who, alarmingly, can do all of these things. The more acute the experience, the less articulate its expression. [13]

Attempts to read a social commitment into Pinter are probably untenable in view of Pinter's unshakable focus on the situation in itself, placing him close to Chekhov. Plausible alternatives to his characters' predicaments are missing, either directly or obliquely. Pinter has no theory of political or social change; what he has is a vision of characters near the ends of their tether.

The Caretaker (1959) was Pinter's first popular success. As in *The Room*, the setting is confined and hemmed in. The play takes place entirely in a room filled with junk collected by Aston, a kindly and slow-witted putterer. For obscure reasons, he has rescued an elderly, irascible malcontent from a beating and given him temporary lodging. His brother Mick, we gradually learn, resents the old man's presence and tries, under the guise of friendship, to prove Davies (as he calls himself) unworthy of Aston's consideration. In terms of subtext, Davies is induced to play the roles of dutiful child to Mick's father and jealous sibling in rivalry with Aston. The problem of verification which touched all the characters in *The Room* and *The Birthday Party* here mostly concerns Davies: his real name and past history. Aston's strange detachment is perhaps too fully explained by a long monologue which he delivers about electric shock treatment, forcefully administered with his mother's permission to end his visionary trances. Now he is preoccupied mostly with someday building a shed in the disused garden out behind the house, a project for which he is collecting tools and bits of lumber. Mick, however, plays games with the old man to disorient and confuse him. After surprising Davies, whom he has been secretly watching, Mick throws him to the ground and subjects him to a barrage of apparently meaningless reminiscences, questions and legal jargon:

> I've got the van outside, I can run you to the police station in five minutes, have you in for trespassing, loitering with intent, daylight robbery, filching, thieving and stinking the place out. What do you say? Unless you're really keen on a straightforward purchase.[14]

Comic by-play over Davies's bag and a hilarious chase of the old man through darkness by a disembodied electrolux leads unpredictably to Mick's offer of a caretaker's job to Davies.

Ironically, Davies unknowingly brings about his own downfall. Paranoid, bigoted, spiteful, and malevolent in his pride, he takes too little "care" about his own security, drawing a knife on Aston when he complains about Davies' sleep-talking. When Davies in turn attacks Aston in Mick's presence, he is abruptly turned out, an act of dispossession which assumes, in Esslin's words, "almost the cosmic proportions of Adam's expulsion from Paradise." [15] Acknowledging the audience's laughter at the play, Pinter recognized the farcical impact of its action but warned that it was funny "only up to a point," [16] and it was because of this point that he wrote the play. It is tragicomic that Davies should direct such hostility toward the distant Aston while becoming, unknowingly, a similar target for Mick, accounting for much of the play's effect of mingled pathos, horror, and ludicrousness. To the audience, seeing so much effort spent on so little is comic. But to the characters, living on the edge of desperation, the trivial prizes at stake assume a transcendent importance. The shifting roles of victim and persecutor, the characters' inability to harmonize their thoughts with either basic desires or verbalizations of them, are typical of Pinter's practice. Quite rational himself, he has envisaged in his drama a variety of clashing, intermingled failures to distinguish between subjective and objective states resembling schizophrenic crises. Quite frequently, with Stanley in *The Birthday Party*, Edward in *The Slight Ache*, Disson in *The Tea Party*, Aston at one time, characters are driven near or over the edge of madness. Often he embraces psychosis as a welcome refuge, tacitly accepting his tormentor's estimate of him.

Throughout his career, Pinter's versatility in the performing arts has been considerable. After establishing himself as one of England's best dramatists, he has continued to act and direct, while providing perceptive critical insights into his own plays. He has moved easily between the media of stage, radio, television, and movies in a series of notable adaptations of his own work and that of others, writing for television such works as *The Dwarfs* (1960), based on an earlier unpublished novel of his, *The Collection* (1961), *The Lover* (1964), and *The Tea Party* (1965). Unlike Arden and Wesker, who have failed to merge well-financed companies, innovative plays, and working-class audiences in sustained endeavors, Pinter has developed his creative talents within existing media.

The Homecoming (1965) is Pinter's most complex and suggestive play, as well as his most recent full-length one. Within a quarreling, loosely-connected family, a rootless group of fathers, brothers, and sons worked out their resentments and fantasies. The title refers ambiguously to Teddy's return with his wife after six years' absence in America, along with his wife Ruth's restoration to homeland and her center in a reconstructed "home." The living-room setting, generational relationships, and the characters' elliptic and deliberately opaque speech are naturalistic. Only a context of prevailing assumptions is missing. The seventy-year-old father, Max, is authoritarian, bitter, and sentimental; one moment his dead wife Jessie had "a heart of gold and a mind," and the next, he remembers her as a "slutbitch." His brother Sam is bitchy and ineffectual but virtuous. Max's three sons are all cold, destructive, and rootless. Teddy, who has become a professor of philosophy, reduces people to objects and ideas, mostly irrelevant. Joey works out his hostility as a daytime demolition worker and aspiring nighttime boxer. Lenny is a pimp who, like Mick, uses language to entrap and confuse, manipulating others more lost than he is himself.

Max's description of Ruth first as "a filthy scrubber off the streets" and then as "a lovely daughter-in-law" indicates a basic uncertainty toward the woman's role in a family which Ruth deliberately exploits. Ironically, the characters lack verifiable pasts or consistent motives apart from their struggle within the family. Lenny's attempts to dominate and undermine Ruth's self-possession are turned against him with a simple hand prop. As she takes a glass of water from him, inviting him first to sit in her lap and then have water poured down his throat, his anecdotes of female conquest grow increasingly bizarre and violent; she is making "some kind of proposal," he realizes. Teddy's vision of a prosperous and happy life in America is immediately challenged; to Ruth, America was all sand and rock, with lots of insects. By kissing Lenny and then taking Joey upstairs as Teddy stands mute, she undercuts the decorum traditionally attached to the role of mother-hood. Rising to petty retaliation, Teddy steals Lenny's cheese roll. In a protest whose point complements his sordid profession, Lenny eloquently mocks the inspiration provided by a family to integral members, "a bit of grace, a bit of je ne sais quoi, a bit of generosity of mind, a bit of liberality of spirit, to reassure us." The rules of family behavior are binding, however, only so long as its members accept them; the corrupt, animalistic drives of all the men suggests that for them, the family and its conventions involves only a conflict of wills, a struggle in which each attempts to impose his subjective vision on the others.

Ruth as the source of fantasy and lust is the focus of the play. Manipulating the others through a sexual magnetism, she creates a radical discrepancy between human will and its effective exercise:

> Look at me. I . . . move my leg. That's all it is. But I wear . . . underwear . . . which moves with me . . . it . . . captures your attention. Perhaps you misinterpret. The action is simple. It is a leg . . . moving. My lips move. Why don't you restrict . . . your observations to that? Perhaps the fact that they move is more significant . . . than the words which come through them.

Her passionless objectivity is symptomatic of the alienation she shares with the other characters. But one of the primary themes of the play is that the essence of woman is her elusive variety, protean and tantalizing in its changeability, captivating in its passivity, yet free. In her acceptance of the family's plan to make her one of Lenny's whores, leaving her enough time for servicing them, she drives a hard bargain. Her response casts doubt on the effectiveness of the strategems a male family has devised to imprison her in their categories. No matter which role she adopts, whether it be mother, prostitute, housekeeper, or temptress, Ruth plays it to perfection, withholding an inner being from judgment altogether. Mask and self neither confirm nor contradict one another, nor as in Pirandello, is the link possibly available but excluded; it is unknowable. The plotlessness of the play is perfectly designed to reveal the kaleidoscopic variousness of woman in the imperfect, partial mirrors the men provide.

Reduced to an object by his refusal to discuss philosophy with Lenny, then to a nullity by Ruth's denial of his role of husband, Teddy disappears. Sam collapses in a brilliant *coup de théâtre*, revealing the meaningless fact that Jessie had been unfaithful to Max in the back seat of his taxi, parodying the well-made solution to a riddling plot. Max's sudden fear that Ruth will invert her role to dominate the family, escaping their control, closes the play. His last request for reassurance he is not too old for love goes unanswered.

Pinter's closed, self-contained ironic comedies provide a sharp contrast with the more open forms used by most of his contemporaries, notably Osborne, Whiting, and Arden. Disparate as their dramatic techniques may be, they all treat with skepticism social myths of progress, social reform, and human betterment. Pinter's characters seem dehumanized and robotlike, his settings contingent and isolated, his marvelously idiomatic and metaphoric language operating in a social and cosmic vacuum. Yet the histrionic images of violence, degeneration, sickness, and despair which take shape through his plays are among the most accurate and artistically compelling in the modern theatre.

With the production of Arnold Wesker's *Trilogy* in June and July of 1960, the author achieved sudden prominence as an idealistic, socially committed leader of the new drama movement. He had impeccable working-class credentials and no university training or work in the theatre at all, although he had been deeply impressed by Osborne's *Look Back in Anger*. Through a prolific career, Wesker has drawn heavily on auto-biographical experiences for the naturalistic, rambling plots of his plays. *Chicken Soup with Barley* (1958),[17] the first full-length drama in his trilogy, traces the disintegration of the Kahn family from the heady 1936 riots of Communists against Mosley's Fascist Blackshirts through 1947, when the nominal head of the family, Harry, loses his little remaining vigor through the first of a number of strokes. In the last scene set in 1956, the Wesker persona Ronnie returns home embittered by the crushing of the Hungarian revolt by the Russians. Despite the disappointments of a bland Labor government and betrayals of nationalistic movements by a self-serving Russian dictatorship, Sarah Kahn is "still a Communist." For years her strength and toughness have sustained her family despite her vacillating husband's weakness. Stung by her son's attack, she tells Ronnie, "if you don't care you'll die."

In *Roots* (1959), the second and best part of Wesker's triptych, the country-bred Beatie Bryant returns from her waitress job in London to her family in Norfolk. Deeply impressed by her fiancé Ronnie Kahn's ideas, she verbally assaults her family's cultural poverty. A climactic letter from Ronnie (who never appears) breaks their engagement, helping Beatie stand alone, in Wesker's words, "articulate at last—." *I'm Talking About Jerusalem* (1960) completes the trilogy with a William Morris-inspired return to the country by Ronnie's sister Ada and brother-in-law Dave Simmonds. But their decade-long struggle with uncomprehending friends and relatives, indifferent clients, and bills ends in resigned failure. Dave finally realizes, "I don't count,

Ronnie. Maybe Sarah's right, maybe you can't build on your own." (An early play, *The Kitchen*, 1958, reflects an interlude in Ronnie's and Wesker's life.)

From the outset of his career, Wesker was hailed as a long-awaited proletarian poet of the theatre, acclaim which now seems inspired more by his cultural and political significance than by his artistic achievements. His audacity in attempting to cover in a trilogy the breakdown of socialistic fervor among a whole class over a span of two decades was praised, along with his vision of and fidelity to naturalistic conventions of speech and life-style among his subjects. However, critics such as John Russell Taylor and Lawrence Kitchin injected cautionary notes. His characters were unexceptional and even boring, they felt; his plotting casual and uneven; and his writing, in Robert Brustein's words, "though full of sincerity, is almost completely wanting in art, being crude, zealous, garrulous and naive." [18]

Responding to his own creative urgings and the strictures of his most intelligent critics, Wesker has continued to experiment with new blends of realism and naturalism, turning to other theatrical techniques and subject matter. *Chips with Everything* (1962) pits an intelligent, wealthy and rebellious draftee against an officer class in the R.A.F., who gradually break down the resistance of Wesker's protagonist to joining the Establishment. The play relies far more heavily on exciting action and sensational subject matter than his preceding trilogy, but his officer figures are too schematic to seem typical. *His Own and Golden City* (1964) covers the period between 1926 and 1990; a promising and energetic labor leader grows old watching his integrity, friendships and plans for rebuilding England's urban scene collapse. In the garrulousness of its speeches and thinness of its dramatic conflicts, the play bears an unfortunate resemblance to Shaw's *Back to Methuselah*. The long one-act *The Four Seasons* (1965) which followed is devoid of social implications, dealing rather with a sadomasochistic conflict between a man and woman, though without much tension or clarity of motivation. His most recent play is *The Friends* (1970). Wesker returns to the collapse of an institution for his subject, this time a loose confederation of once-successful artists, as the woman who had provided the group's sense of purpose wastes into death.

More than a decade later, *Roots* still seems representative of Wesker's concerns and achievement. Very possibly, as Taylor suggests, the play stretches a fine one-act into three acts, duplicating Beatie Bryant's first-act conflict with her sister and husband in a second-act clash with her parents. A number of intriguing dramatic possibilities are left undeveloped: an out-of-wedlock pregnancy of Beatie's sister, the goatish escapades of Stan Mann, and a fruitful confrontation between the absent Ronnie and Beatie's family. In the outlines of its plot, *Roots* bears some resemblance to Ibsen's *The Wild Duck* and O'Neill's *The Iceman Cometh* (though Wesker had not read them). A self-sufficient, closely linked but isolated group is approached by a familiar, possibly superior outsider with a message. After a series of increasingly bitter skirmishes, the intruder departs, perhaps having gained a convert, leaving the group the same or worse off than before. Like Gregers Werle and Ted Hickman, Beatie has returned to her family after an absence of several years. She had fallen in love with Ronnie Kahn in a restaurant where they both had worked. As a result, she quotes his ideas, though with more interest in matrimony than growth of intellect, to prepare her family for his arrival and expose her family's lack of awareness, their acceptance of social injustice, and their preference for third-rate art. Although the Beale's social isolation seems atypical, their characters mix virtues and vices convincingly. They are unembarrassed by discussions of death, perversion, or decay, unpredictably mean and generous, petty and tolerant by turns, with depths of hostility below their acceptance of insult and injustice. Beatie's attempts to replace pop songs with Bizet and radio news headlines with *Guardian* commentaries may involve middle-class snobbery toward their cultural "inferiors," though to do Wesker justice, his characters are more complex than their ideas or their idiomatic Norfolk clichés. In the letter which provides the play's well-made climax, Ronnie writes:

> It wouldn't really work would it? . . . Most of us intellectuals are pretty sick and neurotic—as you have often observed—and we couldn't build a world even if we were given the reins of government—not yet at any-rate.

Faced with Beatie's accusing recriminations, Mrs. Bryant denounces first her daughter and then family:

> Blaming me all the time! . . . Thinks I like it being cooped up in this house all day. Well I'm telling you my gal—I don't! There! And if I had a chance to be away working somewhere the whole lot on you's could go to hell—the lot on you's.

Beatie finally realizes that, "Well, Ronnie's right—it's our own bloody fault. We want the third-rate—we got it! We got it! We got it! We . . ." As her family eats, oblivious to her suffering, she finally realizes she has achieved a selfhood independent of Ronnie's urgings.

Whether Beatie has in fact transcended her past to achieve a more self-assured level of awareness is open to question. Her new language sounds much like Ronnie's, and the pathos of her rejection by family and lover coerces the audience's sympathy. Vivid and bold as the play's conception is, Wesker's inability to move beyond its dramatic assumptions indicates that his limitations as a playwright are fairly deeply ingrained. Too intelligent not to see the flaws and self-deception behind any set of motives or beliefs, he is also too insecure not to crave a cluster of myths grouped loosely under "socialism." Thus Wesker denies his characters the strength of will and latitude of freedom within his plays he himself exercises as creator and citizen. In this regard, his resemblance to Clifford Odets, who never fulfilled his great promise as visionary prophet of social revolution, is rather close.

John Whiting is not really part of the group of playwrights following Osborne into the theatre, but his career overlaps theirs. He began writing in 1947, had his first production with the highly controversial *Saint's Day* in 1951, left the theatre entirely for seven years after subsequent plays encountered similar hostility, and finally returned at Peter Hall's invitation in 1960 to adapt Huxley's *The Devils of Loudun*. His first popular success was also his last play, for he died in 1963. Since he was forced to support himself almost entirely by authoring radio and numerous movie scripts, Whiting has left a rather slight theatre production behind: some unfinished and apprentice work, three short plays and four major works. He has much in common with Arden, though. Whiting is more sharply focused and academic but both indulge a fondness for historical parable, tend to suggest rather than directly present the agonizings of their characters and burden their audiences with demands for thought and tolerance. Good and evil are finally unidentifiable, however vigorously they clash. At the same time, Whiting's characters are more deeply and irrevocably split than Arden's: their roles are more provisional and masklike, their speech poetic by pressure of circumstance (after Arden had shaken off Eliot's influence). Arden's balladlike irruptions into another plane of existence have a counterpart in the sudden descents into self-recognition of Whiting's characters. The idiomatic ruminations of Whiting's people, seeking some overriding encapsulations of fulfillment, provide a foretaste of Beckett and Pinter without gaining their audiences.

The choice of a priest as his protagonist in *The Devils* (1961), Whiting's first use of a religiously oriented figure, is a continuation of his interest in mock-heroic archetypes. Previously he had surrounded the rejected poet Paul Southman with failed painter and admiring critic in *Saint's Day*, dealt with a would-be impersonator of Napoleon in *A Penny For a Song* (1951), and introduced a ruined general in *Marching Song* (1952). Like the use of messianic heroes by Eliot in *Murder in the Cathedral* and Shaw in *Saint Joan*, Whiting's treatment mixes seriousness with irony, savagery with farce. All the themes critics discovered in his earlier plays reemerge in *The Devils*: man's obsession with self-destruction, the need for love, society as a jungle. At the center of his plot is Urbain Grandier, an ambitious, brilliant, and lecherous young vicar appointed to the church of Loudun in the early seventeenth century. The world of the play and its enormous, varied cast are spread out in a Brechtian epic panorama, although such issues as priestly celibacy, the encroachments of centralized government upon local prerogatives, and religious hypocrisy are neither firmly grounded in history nor universalized.

Behind the magnetism and appeal of his personality, Grandier is and feels himself to be an impostor. Though others view him as split between the sensualist and spiritual statesman, his self lacks reality and palpability to him. "I have a great need to be united with God," he explains. "Living has drained the need for life from me. My exercise of the senses has flagged to mere exhaustion. I am a dead man, compelled to live." [19] Such talk strikes a respondent as obliquely suicidal. And in fact, Grandier seems determined to escape consciousness into the mere existence of objects or transcend it altogether.

To re-create a world of sensuous immediacy, Grandier responds mechanically to sexual blandishments though in Phillipe, the freshest and most innocent of his loves, he senses an affection he tries to extend in a futile wedding ritual. Unable to resist dabbling in the tortuous political maneuverings of the time, he joins local resistance to Richilieu's demands that the city's walls be pulled down: "Conflict attracts me, sir. Resistance compels me," he admits. The freedom of his self to expand into any role, to be anybody in fantasy, recurrently threatens to break down into a loss of real freedom. He acts less than reacting, becoming a man who participates from a sense of desperation, a curiously passive kind of existence without responsibility. Whiting has provided him a kind of alter ego in the figure of the Sewerman, who symbolizes the excremental commonality of man and voices what otherwise would be Grandier's soliloquies.

A sudden, hysterical infatuation with him by a humpbacked prioress, Sister Jeanne, creates a perverse tie between their careers, carrying them both inexorably toward destruction. "Grandier's need to be united with God," Simon Trussler comments, "contrasts ironically with Sister Jeanne's identical desire—in one case a repudiation, in the other a sublimation of sexuality." [20] The deliberate, selfish maneuvers of Grandier's growing band of detractors from town, court, and Church establishments menace him, reach temporary setbacks, and again gather force. Whiting's painstaking accumulation of detail seems Websterian, as does his juxtaposition of a highly individualized protagonist against a historical backdrop so thin as to approach caricature at times.

In a spectacular scene, a royal emissary arrives to observe a display by the sisters of various forms of "possession" to a delighted crowd. The visitor, Henry de Conde, views the nuns' motives with an unshaken skepticism which ironically seals Grandier's doom. "Destroy a man for his opposition, his strength or his majesty," he pleads, "But not for this." Grandier's power to struggle ends with his arrest. The final act crushes his hope, spirit, and body in horrendous tortures which strip him of humanity and grandeur. "There are two things a man should never be asked to do in front of other men," he cries, "Perform with a woman, and suffer in pain." In stark terms, love is paid for at a terrible cost. Like Lear, Grandier faces the shattering possibility that unleashed violence knows no bounds, that "once the machinery of destruction has been let loose," in J.

Stampfer's words, "the partner of his covenant may be neither grace nor the balance of law, but malignity, intransigence, or chaos." [21]

Whiting had just embarked on a new and imaginative stage of his artistic development with *The Devils*, one left tantalizingly incomplete at his death. The achievement which remains testifies to his dedication to an exacting writer's craft.

So brief a study leaves no space for mention of peers and successors to Osborne, Arden, Whiting, Wesker, and Pinter. Whiting prepared the way for Pinter and Beckett on the English stage; Robert Bolt, Harold Pinter, and John Arden continue impressive growth; and Peter Shaffer, Tom Stoppard (*Rosencrantz and Guildenstern Are Dead*), and others have managed to strike out in new directions. Predictably, the English theatre will keep on dividing a minority audience between experimental and popularized drama. In the process, its best playwrights will strain to unite enthusiasts from various classes and backgrounds around a creed or vision of an ever-shifting society and infuse more broadly based media such as films and television with fresh and exciting metaphors of conflict. The movement away from naturalism toward Brechtian techniques, personal myth, and nonnaturalistic language which Taylor observed several years ago still goes on. And the steady though modest subsidies provided London-based and provincial theatres by the national and local governments should give rising new dramatists initial productions and audiences. If the recent British playwrights can keep alive their belief in the viability of drama to infuse health into their communities, modern British drama will go on experimenting and flourishing.

Notes

Introduction

1. "Introduction," *Modern British Dramatists* (Engle-wood Cliffs, N. J., 1968), p. 1.
2. *The Third Voice* (Princeton, 1959), p. 18.
3. *The Idea of a Theatre* (Princeton, 1949), p. 224.

1 – Bernard Shaw

1. "Bernard Shaw and Sean O'Casey," *Queen's Quarterly*, 73 (Spring 1966), 13–34.
2. References to Shaw's dramatic writings are taken from the thirty-six-volume Constable Standard Edition of *The Works of Bernard Shaw* (London, 1930–50), which also includes much of his criticism. Paul Hamblyn Ltd. has published in one volume *The Complete Prefaces of Bernard Shaw* (1965).
3. *Shaw: The Style and the Man* (Middletown, Conn., 1962), p. 153.
4. *The Dynamics of Literary Response* (New York, 1968), p. 250.
5. *The Theatre of Revolt* (New York, 1962), p. 191.
6. *The Idea of a Theatre* (Princeton, 1949), p. 181.
7. Eric Bentley, *Bernard Shaw* (New York, 1947).
8. Elizabeth Sachs and Bernard Stern "Bernard Shaw and His Women," *The British Journal of Medical Psychology* 37, no. 4 (Winter 1964), 345.

2 – Oscar Wilde

1. In *The Artist as Critic*, ed. Richard Ellmann (New York, 1968), p. 320. No authoritative edition of the plays exists.

2. Richard Ellmann, *Eminent Domain* (New York, 1967), p. 21.

3. Quoted by Edmund Bergler, " 'Salome,' the Turning Point in the Life of Oscar Wilde," *Psychoanalytic Review* 43, no. 16 (January 1956), 99.

4. *The Playwright as Thinker* (New York, 1957), p. 141.

5. *The Idea of a Theatre* (Princeton, 1949), p. 148.

6. "A Playboy of the Western World," *Partisan Review* 17 (April 1950), 394.

3–W. B. Yeats

1. References to the drama are taken from *The Collected Plays of W. B. Yeats: New Edition with Five Additional Plays* (New York, 1953). Yeat's criticism of the drama appears in his *The Cutting of an Agate* (New York, 1912); and *Autobiographies* (London, 1955).

2. *The Poet in the Theatre* (New York, 1960), p. 118.

3. Quoted in Frank Kermode, *Romantic Image* (New York, 1957), p. 25.

4–J. M. Synge

1. The definitive edition is J. M. Synge, *Collected Works*, ed. Robin Skelton (London: Oxford University Press). This includes *Poems*, vol. 1, ed. Skelton (1962); *Prose*, vol. 2, ed. Alan Price (1966); and *Plays*, vols. 3–4, ed. Ann Saddlemyer (1968).

2. "The Playboy of the Western World," from *The Plays and Poems of J. M. Synge* (London, 1963), p. 58.

3. *J. M. Synge and Modern Comedy* (Dublin, 1968), p. 17.

4. Cited in Norman Holland, *The Dynamics of Literary Response* (New York, 1968), p. 76.

5–Sean O'Casey

1. Quotations from the plays are taken from Sean O'Casey, *Collected Plays* (London, 1950–51), vol. 1–4, and *The Bishop's Bonfire* (London, 1955).

2. *Sean O'Casey* (New York, 1960), p. 94.

3. Hogan, R. G., *The Experiments of Sean O'Casey* (New York, 1960), p. 37.

4. *The Life of the Drama* (New York, 1965), p. 346.

6–T. S. Eliot and Christopher Fry

1. "The Possibility of a Poetic Drama," *The Sacred Wood* (London, 1920), p. 68.

2. "Poetry and Drama," *On Poetry and Poets* (New York, 1957), p. 87.

3. References to the plays are taken from *The Complete Poems and Plays: 1909–1950* (New York, 1952); *The Confidential Clerk* (New York, 1954); and *The Elder Statesman* (New York, 1959).

4. *For Lancelot Andrewes: Essays on Style and Order* (London, 1928), p. ix.

5. "Poetry and Drama," p. 76.

6. *The Double Agent* (New York, 1935), p. 202.

7. "Wordsworth and the Rabbis," *The Opposing Self* (New York, 1955), p. 146.

8. *The Third Voice* (Princeton, 1959), p. 119.

9. "Progression of Theme in Eliot's Modern Plays," *Kenyon Review* 18, no. 3 (Summer 1956), 342.

10. Christopher Fry's publisher is Oxford University Press.

7–Osborne, Arden, Pinter, Wesker and Whiting

1. (Baltimore, Md., 1963), p. 36.

2. John Osborne's publisher in England is Faber & Faber.

3. John Arden's publisher in the United States is Grove Press; in England it is Methuen.

4. "Brecht and the English Theatre," *Tulane Drama Review* 11, no. 4 (Winter 1966), 70.

5. "Arden's Unsteady Ground," *Tulane Drama Review* 11, no. 4 (Winter 1966), 56.

6. "John Arden and the Absurd," *Review of English Literature* 7, no. 4 (Winter 1966), 47–48.

7. "John Arden and the Public Stage," *Cambridge Quarterly* 4, no. 3 (Summer 1969), 226.

8. Quoted in Martin Esslin, *The Theatre of the Absurd* (Garden City, N. Y., 1961), p. 199.

9. Ibid., p. xix.

10. "Pinter and Chekhov: The Bond of Naturalism," *Tulane Drama Review*, 13, no. 2 (Winter 1968), 145.

11. "*The Homecoming*," *Tulane Drama Review* 11, no. 2 (Winter 1966), 186.

12. "The World of Harold Pinter," *Tulane Drama Review* 6, no. 3 (March 1962), 67–68.

13. Quoted in Esslin, *The Theatre of the Absurd*, p. 206.

14. Pinter's publisher in America is Grove Press; in England it is Methuen.

15. *The Theatre of the Absurd*, p. 211.

16. Ibid., p. 212.

17. Wesker's publishers in England have been Jonathan Cape and Penguin; in America, Random House has published his plays.

18. "The English Stage," *New Statesman* 70 (August 6, 1965), 193.

19. Whiting's publisher in England has been Heinemann; in America his *Collected Plays* have been published in two volumes in 1969.

20. "The Plays of John Whiting," *Tulane Drama Review* 11, no. 2 (Winter 1966), 150.

21. "The Catharsis of King Lear," in *Shakespeare: Modern Essays in Criticism*, ed. Leonard Dean (New York, 1967), p. 375.

Selected Bibliography

Bentley, Eric. *Bernard Shaw*. New York, 1957.

Donoghue, Denis. *The Third Voice: Modern British and American Verse Drama*. Princeton, 1959.

Downer, Alan S. *The British Drama*. New York, 1950.

Esslin, Martin. *The Peopled Wound: The Work of Harold Pinter*. New York, 1970.

Gilman, Richard. "Arden's Unsteady Ground," *Tulane Drama Review* 11 (Winter 1966), 54–62.

Krause, David. *Sean O'Casey: The Man and His Work*. New York, 1960.

Ohmann, Richard M. *Shaw: The Style and the Man*. Middletown, Conn., 1962.

Price, Alan. *Synge and Anglo-Irish Drama*. London, 1961.

Ribalow, Harold U. *Arnold Wesker*. New York, 1966.

Roy, Emil. *Christopher Fry*. Carbondale, Ill., 1968.

San Juan, Epifanio, Jr. *The Art of Oscar Wilde*. Princeton, 1967.

Smith, Carol H. *T. S. Eliot's Dramatic Theory and Practice*. Princeton, 1963.

Taylor, John Russell. *Anger and After*. Baltimore, 1963.

Trussler, Simon. *The Plays of John Osborne*. London, 1969.

——. "The Plays of John Whiting," *Tulane Drama Review*. 11 (Winter 1966), 141–51.

Ure, Peter. *Yeats the Playwright*. New York, 1963.

Index

The resurgence of British drama at the end of the nineteenth century brought back to the theatre the vitality it had enjoyed in Shakespeare's age and during the Restoration. Emil Roy traces the history of this resurgence, beginning with G. B. Shaw and including the avant-garde dramatists of the 1960s.

Led by Yeats and Shaw, the Anglo-Irish playwrights of the 1890s created experimental theatres hospitable to their drama. Bernard Shaw's dominance of modern high comedy is indisputable, Roy illustrates, even though he sought political and intellectual influence rather than artistic fame. Most important in Shaw's drama is the passion with which characters identify with ideas, using dialogue to dominate or fend off a threatening antagonist. Oscar Wilde's prominence as Shaw's rival in comedy rests on a single masterpiece, *The Importance of Being Earnest.* Wilde maintains a dandiacal pose from which he comments ironically on a "serious" world.

W. B. Yeats and John Synge chose to represent the idiom of the Irish peasant; however, Yeats's people are stripped to their abstract humanity whereas Synge's are more realistic and vital. Yeats is a rigorous ironist, relying on traditional symbolism, aristocratic nostalgia, and a rudimentary stage. While Synge deals with timeless myths, Sean O'Casey, often regarded as his opposite, depicts current problems. An urban primitivist, O'Casey is deeply committed to the power of impassioned, idiomatic speech to reform society.

The drama of T. S. Eliot is designed to revive an antinaturalistic tradition, with lyric verse considered the basis of drama. Eliot is a rebel questing for community and finding sainthood incompatible with the ways of the world. Christopher Fry is Eliot's closest disciple in poetic drama, but his approach is more panoramic and historical.

A second wave of innovative and rebellious drama swept into the theatre in May 1956 with the premiere of John Osborne's *Look Back in Anger.* It opened the floodgates for a remarkable group of dramatists including Harold Pinter, Arnold Wesker, John Arden,